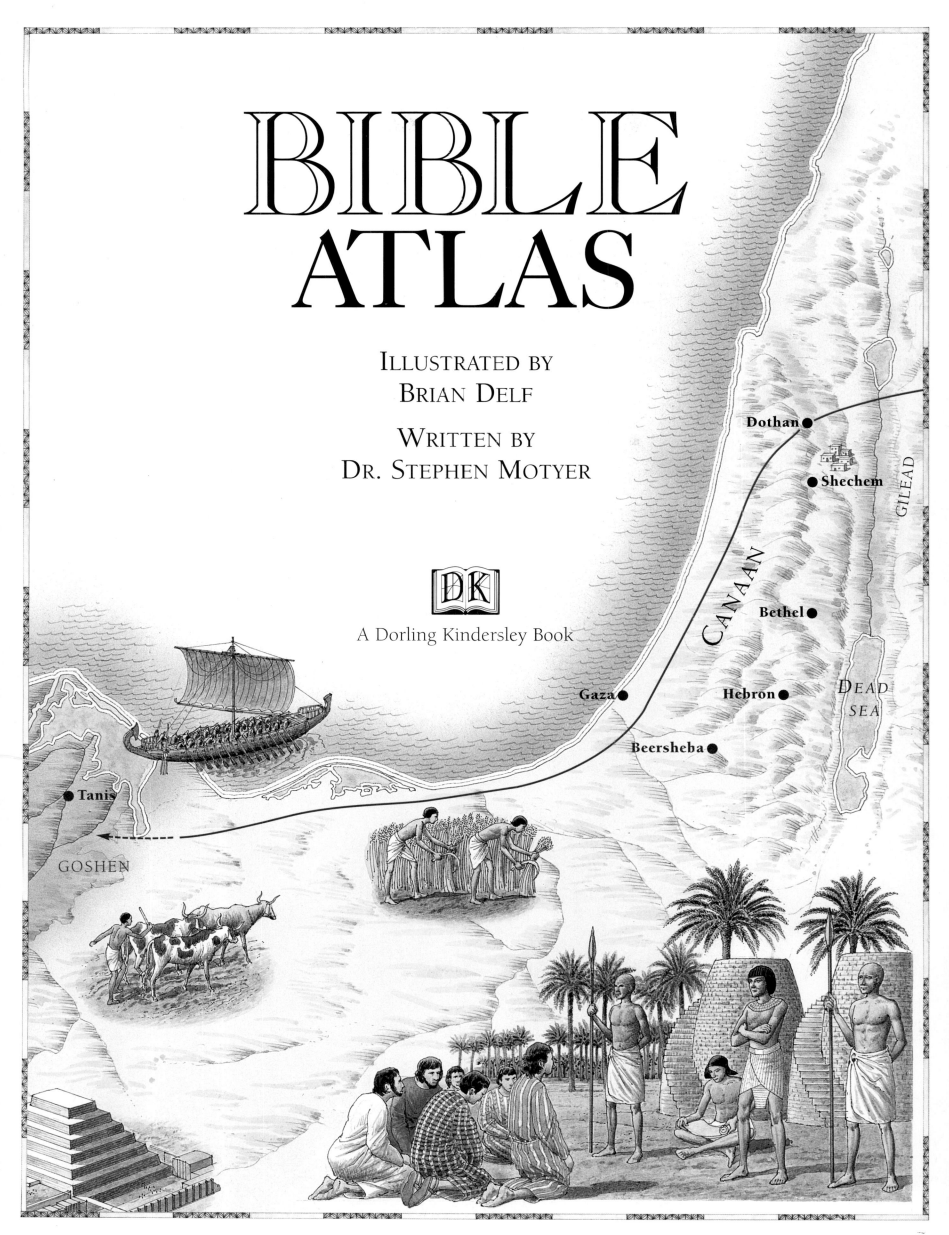

BIBLE ATLAS

ILLUSTRATED BY
BRIAN DELF

WRITTEN BY
DR. STEPHEN MOTYER

DK

A Dorling Kindersley Book

Dothan

Shechem

GILEAD

CANAAN

Bethel

DEAD SEA

Gaza

Hebron

Beersheba

Tanis

GOSHEN

LONDON, NEW YORK, SYDNEY, DELHI, PARIS, MUNICH, and JOHANNESBURG

Project Editor Sadie Smith
US Editors Claudia Volkman, David Barrett
Project Art Editor Polly Appleton
Senior Editor Marie Greenwood
Publishing Manager Jayne Parsons
Managing Art Editor Jacquie Gulliver
DTP Designers Andrew O'Brien, Matthew Ibbotson
Picture Research Jo Haddon
Jacket Design Dean Price
Production Kate Oliver, Jenny Jacoby

Additional text by Philip Wilkinson

First American Edition 2001
00 01 02 03 04 05 10 9 8 7 6 5 4 3 2 1

Published in the United States by DK Publishing, Inc.,
95 Madison Avenue, New York, New York 10016

Published in Great Britain by Dorling Kindersley Limited

Scriptural quotations are taken from the *Holy Bible*, New Living Translation, copyright © 1996. Used by
permission of Tyndale House Publishers Inc., Wheaton, Illinois. All rights reserved.

ISBN 0-7894-7872-2

Library of Congress Cataloging-in-Publication Data

Motyer, Stephen, 1950-
 Bible atlas / by Stephen Motyer ; illustrated by Brian Delf.-- 1st
American ed.
 p. cm.
 ISBN 0-7894-7872-2
 1. Bible--Geography--Maps. [1. Bible--Geography--Maps.] I. Delf,
Brian, ill. II. Title.
 G2230 .M7 2001
 220.91'022'3--dc21

 2001018239

Reproduced by Dot Gradations, Essex, UK
Printed and bound by Artes Graficas Toledo, Spain
D.L. TO: 618 - 2001
See our complete catalog at

www.dk.com

CONTENTS

DISCOVERING THE WORLD OF THE BIBLE

THE BIBLE IS AN AMAZING COLLECTION of 66 books which tells the dramatic story of God's relationship with the human race. It is divided into the Old and New Testaments, both of which contain different kinds of writings – history, teachings, poetry, even songs. Most of the events in the Bible take place in and around the Holy Land, known at different times as Canaan, the Promised Land, Judah, and Israel. Using ancient artifacts and current archaeological research, the major stories of the Bible are shown here in their historical and geographical context.

FINE CARVING
This ivory carving of a winged, human-headed creature called a sphinx, is thought to have been made by Phoenician artists. It was found near the ancient Assyrian capital of Nimrud and dates from the 8th or 9th century BC.

Detail from a 6th century AD mosaic showing the walled city of Jerusalem.

THE BIBLE LANDS

MOST OF THE EVENTS IN THE BIBLE took place in the region to the east of the Mediterranean Sea, known as the Holy Land. A huge arc of rich farming land, called the Fertile Crescent, stretched all the way from here to Mesopotamia – birthplace of Abraham and site of some of the world's first major cities, including Ur and Babylon. Further east was Persia (now called Iran). To the southwest of the Holy Land lies Egypt, where a great civilization flourished during Old Testament times. Most people in the Old Testament did not travel outside this area and knew nothing of the world beyond it. By the time of the New Testament, the Holy Land was ruled by the Romans, whose mighty empire stretched from Italy right around the Mediterranean Sea.

MAP OF THE WORLD

AREA SHOWN
ON LARGE MAP

WORLD OF THE BIBLE
The events of the Old Testament took place in the region that is today made up of Israel, Syria, Jordan, Lebanon, Iran, Iraq, and Egypt. Many New Testament stories occurred in the countries to the north and east of the Mediterranean Sea, including Turkey and Greece. The Holy Land, God's promised land of Canaan, lies at the heart of both the Old and New Testaments. On this map the names of towns and cities in the Bible are shown alongside modern country names and borders. Many of the places mentioned in the Bible still exist today.

THE JUDEAN DESERT
The Judean Desert lies to the west of the Dead Sea. It is one of several desert regions in the Bible. Its landscape ranges from craggy chalk hills to low-lying areas near the Dead Sea. The climate is hot, with very little rain and a strong, dry wind. Strange rocky outcrops remain where the winds have worn away the surrounding stone. This is the "wilderness of Judea" of the New Testament. It has probably changed little from the days when John the Baptist preached here.

MESOPOTAMIAN MARSHLAND
The Tigris and Euphrates are the two great rivers of Mesopotamia. The rivers join north of Basra to form the Shatt-al-Arab (River of the Arabs), which flows into the Persian Gulf. The country here is marshy, with small islands of dry land among streams, canals, and boggy areas. These patches of land are now home to the Ma'dan people (sometimes called the Marsh Arabs). They live by catching waterfowl and herding water buffalo, and build houses from reeds. The Israelites were later exiled to this region. It is possible that this was also the location of the Garden of Eden.

FARMING IN THE NILE DELTA
Ancient Egypt depended entirely on the life-giving waters of the Nile River. Every year in September the river would rise and flood the land on either side, depositing new rich soil from upstream. The Nile Delta, at the mouth of the river, was formed entirely of this rich soil and was very fertile.

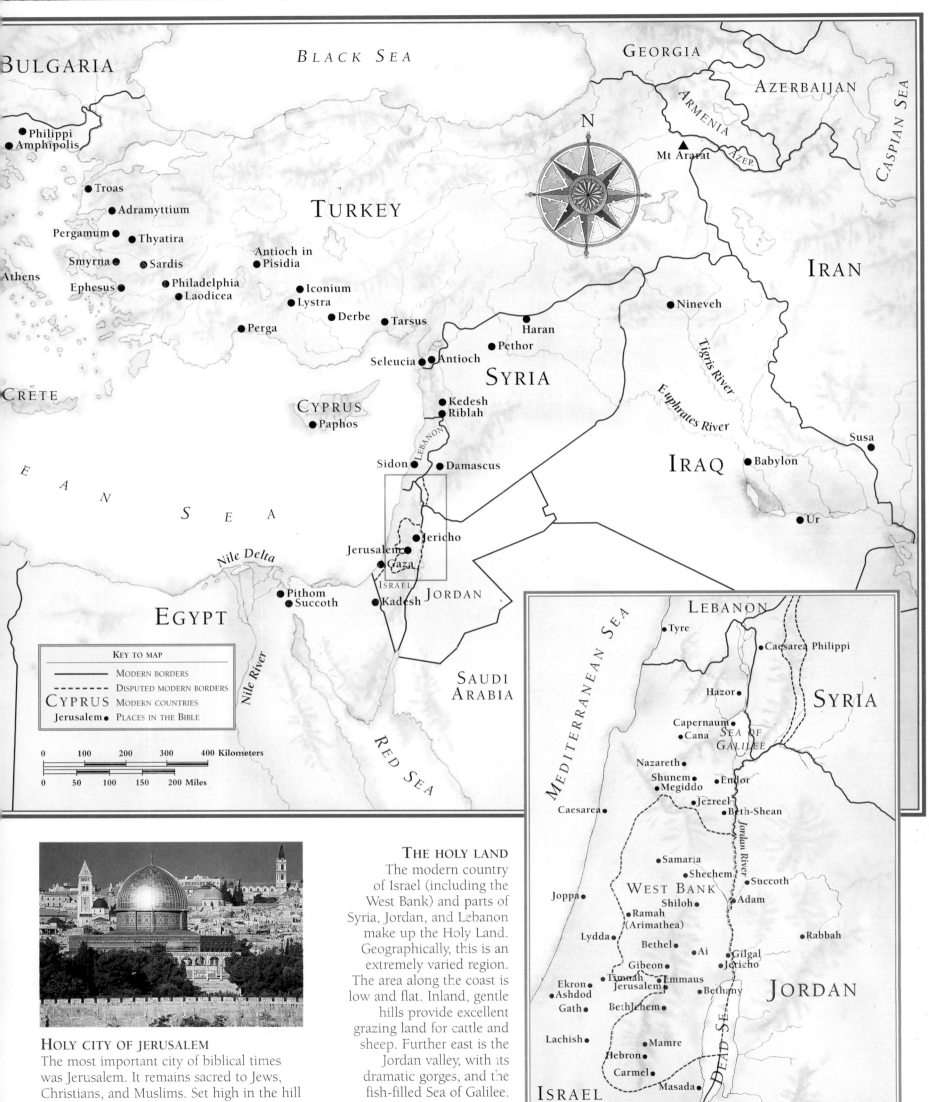

Map labels (main map)

BULGARIA

BLACK SEA

GEORGIA

AZERBAIJAN

• Philippi
• Amphipolis

N

Mt Ararat ▲

ARMENIA

AZER.

CASPIAN SEA

• Troas
• Adramyttium

TURKEY

Pergamum • • Thyatira

IRAN

Smyrna • • Sardis

Athens •

Antioch in Pisidia •

Ephesus • • Philadelphia
  • Laodicea

• Iconium
• Lystra

• Derbe

• Tarsus

• Nineveh

• Haran

• Pethor

CRETE

• Perga

Seleucia • • Antioch

SYRIA

Tigris River

Euphrates River

CYPRUS

• Paphos

• Kedesh
• Riblah

Susa •

E A N

LEBANON

IRAQ

• Babylon

N

Sidon • • Damascus

S E A

• Ur

Nile Delta

• Jericho

Jerusalem •
  • Gaza

ISRAEL JORDAN

• Pithom
• Succoth

EGYPT

• Kadesh

SAUDI ARABIA

KEY TO MAP

———	MODERN BORDERS
- - - -	DISPUTED MODERN BORDERS
CYPRUS	MODERN COUNTRIES
Jerusalem •	PLACES IN THE BIBLE

0   100   200   300   400 Kilometers

0   50   100   150   200 Miles

Nile River

RED SEA

HOLY CITY OF JERUSALEM

The most important city of biblical times was Jerusalem. It remains sacred to Jews, Christians, and Muslims. Set high in the hill country of Judah, it became the Israelites' capital city. At the center of Jerusalem was the sacred Jewish Temple. Only the Western, or Wailing, Wall of the Temple remains.

THE HOLY LAND

The modern country of Israel (including the West Bank) and parts of Syria, Jordan, and Lebanon make up the Holy Land. Geographically, this is an extremely varied region. The area along the coast is low and flat. Inland, gentle hills provide excellent grazing land for cattle and sheep. Further east is the Jordan valley, with its dramatic gorges, and the fish-filled Sea of Galilee. Beyond the Jordan River lies a flat plateau, while to the southwest is the parched Negev desert.

Inset map (The Holy Land)

MEDITERRANEAN SEA

LEBANON

• Tyre

• Caesarea Philippi

SYRIA

• Hazor

Capernaum •
• Cana

SEA OF GALILEE

Nazareth •

Shunem • • Endor
• Megiddo

• Jezreel

Caesarea •

• Beth-Shean

Jordan River

• Samaria
  • Shechem

• Succoth

Joppa •

WEST BANK

• Adam

• Shiloh

Lydda •

• Ramah (Arimathea)

• Rabbah

• Bethel

• Ai

• Gilgal

Gibeon • • Jericho

Ekron • • Timnah • Emmaus

Ashdod • Jerusalem • • Bethany

Gath •

JORDAN

• Bethlehem

Lachish •

DEAD SEA

• Mamre

Hebron •

Carmel •

ISRAEL

• Masada

• Beersheba

NEGEV DESERT

0   40 Kilometers

0   20 Miles

MAPPING THE WORLD OF THE BIBLE

PEOPLE HAVE BEEN MAKING MAPS of the Bible lands for hundreds of years now, but it wasn't until the 19th century that the first accurate maps were made. The geography of this part of the world has always been of great interest to people because of the many important events and journeys which are described in the Bible. Through mapmaking and archaeology, the events of the Bible are made even more vivid. Archaeologists and mapmakers help bring the history of Old and New Testament times to life through studies of the landscape, the objects found, and ancient sites they discover. They investigate how people lived, who ruled, and for how long. With their findings, archaeologists uncover the past and help us to map the world of the Bible in rich detail.

Bethabara, home of John the Baptist.

Two boats can be seen sailing on the Dead Sea.

The Jordan River is shown full of fish.

Jericho is depicted as a walled town with many towers.

The Garden of Gethsemane, where Jesus was betrayed.

Jerusalem is shown in great detail. (See page 4–5)

The scrolls were made out of leather.

THE DEAD SEA SCROLLS
In 1947 a Bedouin shepherd boy, wandering near the Dead Sea, threw a stone into the open mouth of a cave above him. He was surprised to hear the sound of breaking pottery. The boy climbed up and found several large jars containing ancient manuscripts. The Dead Sea Scrolls, as they became known, were from the library of a sect (religious group) that had lived nearby at Qumran. Through their writings, we know much more about life at the time of Jesus.

The Dead Sea Scrolls were found rolled up in clay storage jars.

KATHLEEN KENYON
Dame Kathleen Kenyon (1906–1978) was one of the greatest archaeologists of the last century. She excavated sites in Britain, Africa, and Italy, as well as in Israel. In the 1950s, Kathleen was the director of the British School of Archaeology in Jerusalem, and she led a famous excavation in Jericho. She mapped the history of Jericho and discovered that it is one of the oldest cities in the world.

BLACK OBELISK
This is one of the carved panels on the side of an Assyrian monument known as the Black Obelisk. It shows King Jehu of Israel, who is introduced in the Second Book of Kings in the Bible, bowing before King Shalmaneser III of Assyria in 841 BC. The Black Obelisk was discovered at Nimrud in 1846 by archaeologist Henry Layard. It is over 6 ft (2 m) high and is now kept in the British Museum in London.

A figure kneels to pay tribute.

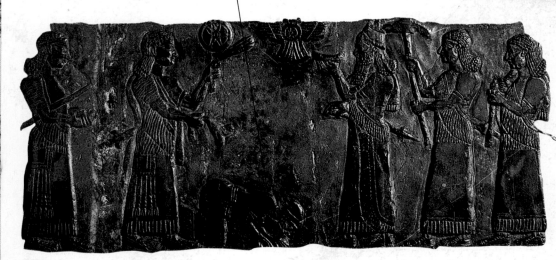

THE MADABA MOSAIC MAP

This remarkable mosaic was damaged by people who did not realize how important it was, long before it was recognized and preserved by archaeologists. It is on display in the church of St. George at Madaba, Jordan, and was probably made around AD 550. The Jordan River flows across the map from the left (north) to the Dead Sea in the middle. On the right (south) we can see the Nile Delta in Egypt. The writing on the map is Greek.

Beersheba is placed accurately in the western Negev Desert.

Gaza, once a major port, is shown in some detail.

The Nile is shown flowing from east to west, rather than south to north, as it is in reality.

THE PALESTINE EXPLORATION FUND

The Palestine Exploration Fund (PEF) was founded in 1865 to study the geography, history, and people of the Bible lands. Many famous archaeologists have worked for the Fund, investigating the history of Bible cities and sites. Charles Warren was one of the first to study the archaeology of Jerusalem and the Temple Mount, between 1867–1870. The above map, made by the PEF, is one of the first accurate maps ever made of Palestine. It is one of a series of 26 maps made during the Survey of Western Palestine (1871–1878).

EXCAVATIONS AT MASADA

Situated near the Dead Sea, Masada is one of the most famous archaeological sites in Israel (see page 35). By AD 70, Jewish resistance to the invading Romans had almost been crushed. Masada, a large settlement inhabited by Jewish rebels, was the last to fall. It is here that about 1,000 Jewish men, women, and children held back the mighty Roman army for three years (AD 70–73). Eventually, they all committed suicide rather than be captured.

The excavated site of a mikve – the bathing area where the Jewish people of Masada performed their purification (washing) ceremonies.

MAPPING EVERYDAY LIFE

Archaeologists work like detectives, putting together clues to create an overall picture of people and their lives. They discover how people lived from day-to-day when they dig up household items such as pottery. Archaeologists can also work out trade routes by tracing where things were made to where they were found. Style and fashion changed during Bible times, just like it does today. So, archaeologists can often date a site when they find pottery of a particular type or with patterns that belong to a certain period.

This beautiful jug, made in the shape of a bull, was made in Cyprus and imported to Canaan.

This delicate glass jar was made in Phoenicia, where glassmaking was one of the most important industries.

These are different types of pins, used to fasten clothing. The pin on the right dates from the Persian period, and was called a *fibula*. It bears a resemblance to a modern day safety pin.

THE OLD TESTAMENT

FROM THE RUGGED MOUNTAINS OF SINAI to the salty Dead Sea, the events of the Old Testament took place in some of the world's most dramatic landscapes. On their journey through this terrain, the founders of Israel encountered the barren deserts of the Negev, the thickets and scrub of the Jordan Valley, and the forested hill country of Judah. Their travels brought them into contact with the great centers of early civilization – the ancient settlements of Mesopotamia and Egypt, and the magnificent city of Babylon. During this journey, God led them to create their own nation, centered on the Holy City of Jerusalem.

God's promise to Abraham
The story of the Israelites began with Abraham. God promised Abraham that he would become the father of a great nation and that he would have as many descendants as there are stars in the sky.

Mount Sinai

11

THE JOURNEYS OF THE PATRIARCHS

THE BOOK OF GENESIS describes how Terah embarked on an epic journey with his son Abraham and the rest of his family. They left behind the glittering city of Ur in southern Mesopotamia and traveled northwest to Haran on the fertile plains south of Turkey. As they journeyed from place to place, the family led a nomadic life, herding their sheep and cattle along the banks of the Euphrates River. Many years later, God told Abraham to travel south from Haran to the hill country of Canaan, where he would become "the father of a new nation." Abraham obeyed God's call. He found pasture for his flocks around Hebron, and traveled to Egypt via Beersheba. Abraham's son Isaac, and Isaac's son Jacob were also travelers. On his way back to Canaan from Haran, Jacob had a mysterious meeting with God, who gave him the name Israel. Abraham, Isaac, and Jacob are known as patriarchs, the founding fathers of the nation of Israel.

Abraham's descendants
According to Genesis, God promised Abraham that he would have as many descendants as there are stars in the sky. Abraham and his wife Sarah reached old age without having any children. Finally, God granted them a son, Isaac, who in turn had a son, Jacob. And Abraham's descendants continue even today.

Abraham sacrificed a ram in place of Isaac.

Abraham's test
God told Abraham to take his son Isaac to Moriah (later called Jerusalem). To test Abraham's faith, God ordered Abraham to make the greatest sacrifice of all – to kill Isaac. Abraham was about to carry out God's wishes when an angel appeared and ordered him to stop. Abraham had proved that he placed his love of God before everything.

Abraham may have followed traders or local nomadic tribes on his journey to Canaan.

Jacob disguised himself as his hairy brother Esau by covering his hands and neck with goatskin.

Haran

Halab

Hamath

CANAAN

Damascus

Hazor

M E D I T E R R A N E A N   S E A

Bethel

Moriah (Jerusalem)

Hebron

Beersheba

ABRAHAM'S JOURNEY
JACOB'S JOURNEY

EGYPT

Nile River

THE RUINS OF BEERSHEBA
Archaeologists have unearthed an ancient city at Beersheba, 48 miles (77 km) southwest of Jerusalem. The remains date from the Iron Age (1000–720 BC). Abraham settled here many years earlier. He may have chosen the site because of its southern location and the presence of several wells in the area.

0	40	80	120	160	200 Kilometers
0		40	80		120 Miles

Jacob and Esau
Isaac and his wife Rebekah had twin sons, Jacob and Esau. God promised Rebekah that her favorite son, Jacob, would be Isaac's heir even though Esau was the elder brother. So Jacob and his mother tricked Isaac, who was old and blind, into giving Jacob his blessing. When Esau found out he was furious, and Jacob was forced to flee.

SUMERIAN TREASURE

Made from solid gold, this helmet was one of the objects buried in the royal graves of Ur. It was just one item among hundreds made of costly materials such as silver, gold, and semiprecious stones. These "grave goods" were intended for the king and queen to use in the next world. They show the fabulous wealth of the rulers in this part of southern Mesopotamia, known as Sumer.

Builders used mud bricks to build these distinctive bee-hive shaped houses.

The Sumerians are believed to have invented the wheel, which they used when making pots.

Jacob and Rachel

After tricking Esau, Jacob fled to Haran, where he lived with his uncle Laban, a sheep farmer. Jacob fell in love with Laban's beautiful daughter, Rachel, and Laban promised that they could marry if Jacob worked for him for seven years. When the time was up, Laban fooled Jacob into marrying Rachel's older sister, Leah. Laban finally allowed Jacob to marry Rachel, but Jacob had to promise to work for another seven years.

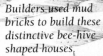

The rivers provided a rich source of fish for the Sumerians.

MESOPOTAMIA

Tigris River

Sumerian craftsmen were renowned for the gold jewelry and ornaments they made for the royal family.

SCENES FROM UR

This stunning wooden box, found in a royal grave, was made in the city of Ur around 2500 BC. The pictures on this side of the box show peacetime scenes from Ur – a royal banquet and a procession of farmers taking cattle and sheep as gifts for the king. Scenes on the other side show the chariots and warriors of the city's army.

The ziggurat at Ur was a huge mud-brick temple dedicated to Nanna, the Sumerian moon god.

Euphrates River

One of the first writing systems was developed by the Sumerians. They wrote on damp clay tablets, which later set hard.

Ur ●

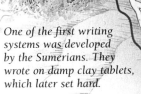

Date palms grew in the salty marshland of Mesopotamia. The Sumerians ate the dates and used the wood to build their homes.

Jacob's ladder

On his way to Haran, Jacob dreamed about a staircase stretching to heaven, with angels walking up and down the steps. In the dream, God spoke to Jacob, promising him that the land where he slept would later be his, and that his children would live there. Jacob named the place Bethel, meaning "House of God."

Sumerian merchants sailed along the coasts of the Persian Gulf, trading in gold, ivory, hardwoods, and precious stones.

THE ISRAELITES IN EGYPT

JACOB AND HIS FAMILY prospered as farmers in Canaan's hill country. Then a terrible famine struck. The book of Genesis tells how Jacob and his sons traveled southwest to Egypt in search of food. There they were reunited with Jacob's favorite son Joseph, who had been sold into slavery in Egypt many years earlier. Joseph had risen to the position of vizier (prime minister) to Pharaoh, the ruler of Egypt. Pharaoh allowed Jacob's family to settle in the north of his land. This was the delta region, where the great Nile River divided into many separate streams. Although there was little rain in this hot country, the streams overflowed into swamps and marshes. The soil was damp and grew rich grass for goats and cattle. Here, over several generations, Jacob's family grew into the twelve tribes of Israel. The Israelites, as cattle farmers, became some of the richest people in Egypt. As time passed they forgot their homeland in Canaan.

Joseph is carried off to Egypt

Jacob gave his favorite son Joseph a beautiful, multicolored coat. This infuriated Joseph's jealous elder brothers, who plotted to get rid of Joseph. One day, while looking after their flocks at Dothan in Canaan, the brothers saw their chance. They threw Joseph down a well, leaving him for dead. Just then a group of spice merchants from Gilead passed by on their way to Egypt. "Let's sell Joseph as a slave," suggested one of the brothers. They dragged him out of the well and sold him to the traders for twenty pieces of silver. As Joseph was taken to Egypt, the brothers smeared his coat with goat's blood and told Jacob that a wild animal had killed his son.

ROUTE OF SPICE MERCHANTS

CANAAN

GILEAD

Shechem

Dothan

After buying Joseph as a slave in Dothan, the merchants continued to Egypt.

ON THE BANKS OF THE NILE

The Nile River was Egypt's lifeline. Every year it flooded, spreading rich mud over the land on either bank. This narrow strip of fertile soil was where most of the Egyptian people lived, growing crops such as wheat and barley. Beyond was parched desert and rock-strewn mountains.

Joseph interprets Pharaoh's strange dream

Years later, Pharaoh had a mysterious dream in which seven thin cows ate up seven fat ones, but grew no fatter. "What could it mean?" wondered Pharaoh. Then the king's cup-bearer remembered that the Israelite slave Joseph was good at interpreting dreams. Joseph told Pharaoh that Egypt would enjoy seven good harvests, followed by seven bad years. This prediction, given to Joseph by God, soon came true. Pharaoh made Joseph his vizier, or prime minister, in charge of storing grain for the years of famine ahead.

Joseph was brought before Pharaoh to explain the Egyptian leader's strange dream.

Ships were powered by both oars and sails. This allowed them to travel at great speed along the Mediterranean coast.

Farmers cut their grain using stone-bladed wooden sickles. The straw was left standing and later made into mats and baskets.

Only the most prosperous farmers could afford herds of cattle. Beef was a luxury meat, eaten by wealthy Egyptians.

The Step Pyramid at Saqqara, tomb of Pharaoh Djoser, was the first of all the pyramids to be built.

A small, lightweight wooden plow, pulled by a pair of cattle, cut easily through Egypt's sandy soil.

DEAD SEA

Hebron ●

Beersheba ●

Gaza ●

● Tanis

Rameses ●

GOSHEN

● Bubastis

● Heliopolis

EGYPT

● Giza

Saqqara ●

● Heracleopolis

Nile River

Shadufs were devices for lifting heavy buckets of water from the Nile. Canals carried the water to distant fields, far from the river.

The Great Pyramid at Giza had stood for hundreds of years by the time the Israelites settled in Egypt.

The Egyptians hunted waterfowl among the reeds of the Nile with boomerang-shaped throw sticks.

100 Kilometers
100 Miles
50
50
50
50
0
0

Joseph meets his brothers

When famine struck Canaan, Joseph's older brothers traveled to Egypt looking for food. Joseph recognized his brothers immediately, but they did not realize it was Joseph because of his fine clothes. Joseph sold them some corn, but told them to come back with their youngest brother, Benjamin. When they returned, Joseph accused Benjamin of stealing so that he would have to stay in Egypt as a slave. Knowing how upset Jacob would be to lose another son, one of the brothers, Judah, begged Joseph to take him as a slave instead. Now Joseph realized his brothers had changed. He could hide his identity no longer and he told his brothers who he was. Then he sent for Jacob and the rest of his family.

Joseph is reunited with his father

Jacob was overjoyed that his favorite son was still alive. Joseph wept with happiness when he saw his father after so many years. After their tearful reunion, they went to see Pharaoh. The Egyptian ruler granted Joseph's people – the Israelites – an area in the land of Goshen, in the eastern delta of the Nile. This was some of the best land in all Egypt. Here the Israelites tended their goats and cattle for generations, living peacefully alongside the Egyptians.

RECORDING THE HARVEST

This colorful Egyptian tomb painting dates from around 1570 BC. It comes from the tomb of Menna in the important Egyptian city of Thebes. The painting shows a group of four scribes recording the harvest using reed pens and rolls of papyrus. Making a record like this informed the pharaoh's officials how much food was available and how much tax they could collect from farmers.

THE FLIGHT FROM EGYPT

LIFE WAS GOOD FOR THE ISRAELITES in the well-watered fields of Goshen, beside the Nile River. However, as time passed, the rulers of Egypt saw the Israelites as a threat and began to use them as slaves on Egypt's great building projects. Then Pharaoh commanded that every Israelite boy should be killed at birth. God saw the Israelites' misery and sent Moses to rescue them. Moses entered Pharaoh's palace with God's demand, "Let my people go!" Pharaoh refused. Ten dreadful plagues then struck Egypt, until Pharaoh gave in and ordered the Israelites to leave. Pharaoh's army chased after the fleeing Israelites and nearly trapped them, but God parted the Red Sea, allowing Moses and his people to cross safely to the other side. From there they traveled south to Mount Sinai where God gave Moses the Ten Commandments. Then the Israelites wandered north across the hot Sinai Desert in the direction of Canaan – the land God had promised Abraham.

PHARAOH OF EGYPT
Rameses II (c. 1285-1215 BC) was a powerful Egyptian king, and many statues of him survive. He may have been the ruler, known in the Bible simply as "Pharaoh," who enslaved the Israelites.

EGYPT

Egyptian scribes kept records for Pharaoh. They also wrote stories and acted like secretaries.

Tanis

Ra'amses

Bubastis

GOSHEN

Heliopolis
Giza

Papyrus reeds grew along the banks of the Nile. Scribes first cut and dried the reeds. Then they wove them into sheets to make paper to write on.

Nile River

Egyptian army chariots could move very quickly into battle. Each chariot had a driver and a soldier. Chariots like these pursued the Israelites to the Red Sea.

Moses in the reeds
Jochebed, an Israelite woman, hid her baby son Moses from Egyptian soldiers for three months after his birth. As Moses grew older, it became more and more difficult to keep him hidden. So, putting her trust in God, Jochebed left her son floating in a papyrus basket on the Nile, near the place where Pharaoh's daughter used to bathe. Moses' sister Miriam hid nearby. Sure enough, the princess found the baby, was touched by his helpless cries – and then unknowingly employed Moses' mother to look after him!

EGYPTIAN BRICKMAKERS
This picture from the wall of a tomb in Thebes shows Egyptian slaves making bricks. The Israelites were also forced to do this backbreaking work. To make bricks, clay was mixed with straw. The straw gave the bricks more strength. The bricks were shaped and set out to dry.

Crossing the Red Sea
When the Israelites left Egypt, Pharaoh immediately regretted letting them go, and sent his army to bring them back. The army caught up with the Israelites at the Red Sea. Trapped between the army and the water, the Israelites were terrified. But Moses held out his staff, and to the Israelites' amazement, God parted the water and they crossed the sea on dry ground.

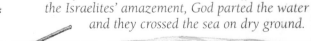

THE PLAGUES OF EGYPT

Moses and his brother Aaron went to Pharaoh to ask for freedom for the Israelites. When Pharaoh refused to let the Israelites leave Egypt, ten plagues struck the country. Each plague was worse than the last, but Pharaoh would not give in. Finally, God told Moses that every first-born child in Egypt would die. However, the Israelites would be spared this terrible plague if they followed God's instructions. They had to smear lamb's blood over their doorposts so God would know to "pass over" their home. At midnight, this devastating plague struck, and at last Pharaoh ordered the Israelites to leave.

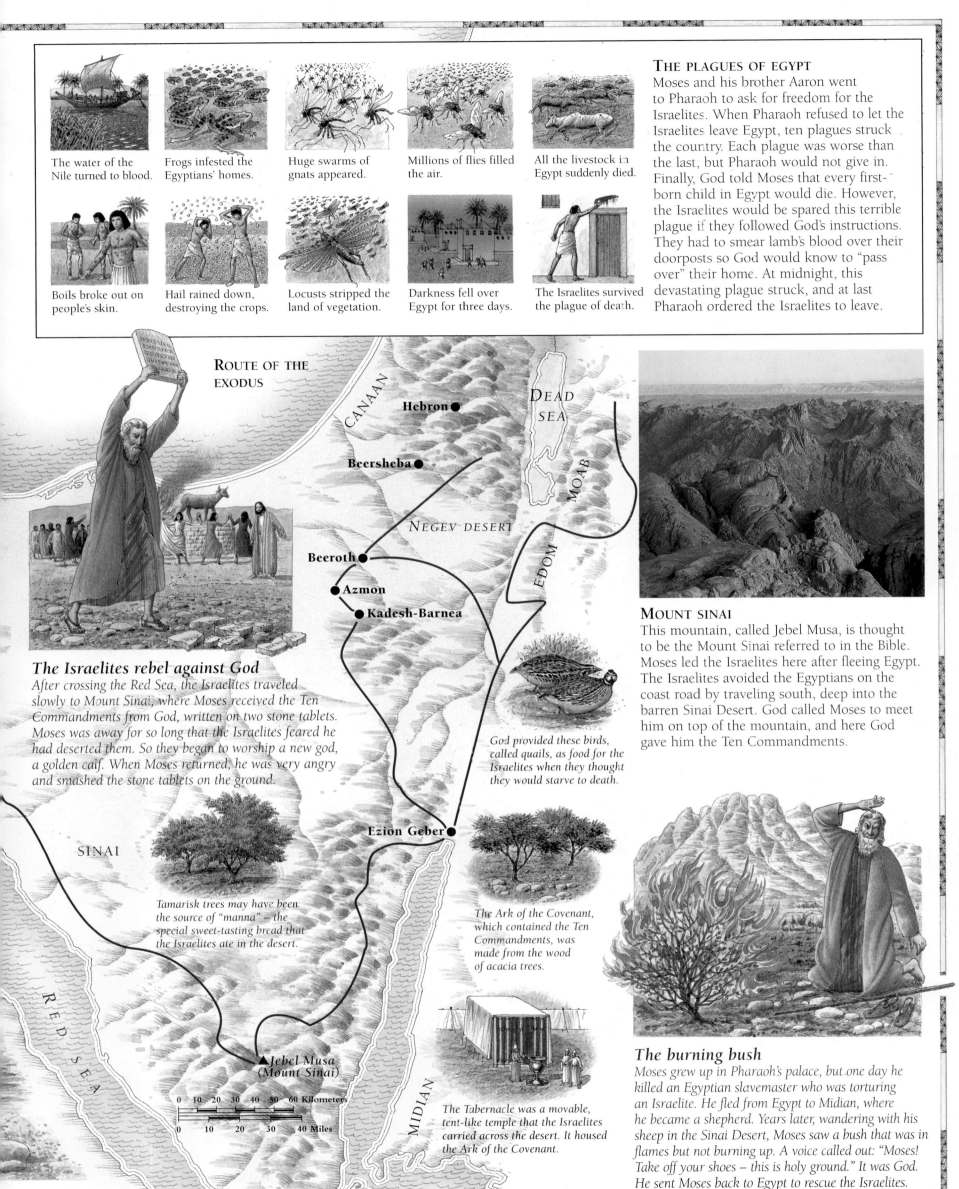

The water of the Nile turned to blood.

Frogs infested the Egyptians' homes.

Huge swarms of gnats appeared.

Millions of flies filled the air.

All the livestock in Egypt suddenly died.

Boils broke out on people's skin.

Hail rained down, destroying the crops.

Locusts stripped the land of vegetation.

Darkness fell over Egypt for three days.

The Israelites survived the plague of death.

ROUTE OF THE EXODUS

The Israelites rebel against God

After crossing the Red Sea, the Israelites traveled slowly to Mount Sinai, where Moses received the Ten Commandments from God, written on two stone tablets. Moses was away for so long that the Israelites feared he had deserted them. So they began to worship a new god, a golden calf. When Moses returned, he was very angry and smashed the stone tablets on the ground.

God provided these birds, called quails, as food for the Israelites when they thought they would starve to death.

Tamarisk trees may have been the source of "manna" – the special sweet-tasting bread that the Israelites ate in the desert.

The Ark of the Covenant, which contained the Ten Commandments, was made from the wood of acacia trees.

The Tabernacle was a movable, tent-like temple that the Israelites carried across the desert. It housed the Ark of the Covenant.

CANAAN

Hebron

DEAD SEA

Beersheba

MOAB

NEGEV DESERT

EDOM

Beeroth

Azmon

Kadesh-Barnea

Ezion Geber

SINAI

▲ Jebel Musa (Mount Sinai)

RED SEA

MIDIAN

0 10 20 30 40 50 60 Kilometers
0 10 20 30 40 Miles

MOUNT SINAI

This mountain, called Jebel Musa, is thought to be the Mount Sinai referred to in the Bible. Moses led the Israelites here after fleeing Egypt. The Israelites avoided the Egyptians on the coast road by traveling south, deep into the barren Sinai Desert. God called Moses to meet him on top of the mountain, and here God gave him the Ten Commandments.

The burning bush

Moses grew up in Pharaoh's palace, but one day he killed an Egyptian slavemaster who was torturing an Israelite. He fled from Egypt to Midian, where he became a shepherd. Years later, wandering with his sheep in the Sinai Desert, Moses saw a bush that was in flames but not burning up. A voice called out: "Moses! Take off your shoes – this is holy ground." It was God. He sent Moses back to Egypt to rescue the Israelites.

17

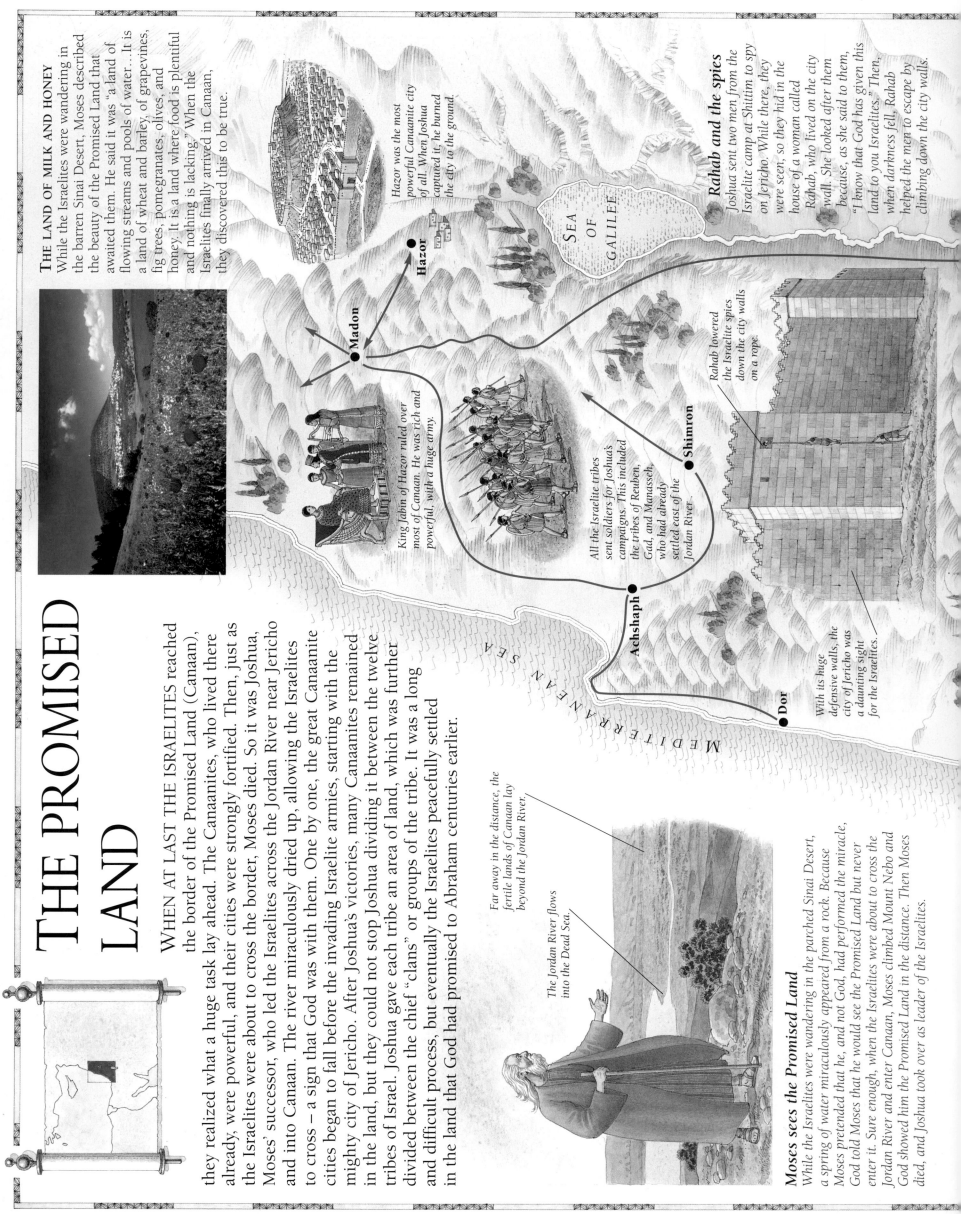

THE PROMISED LAND

WHEN AT LAST THE ISRAELITES reached the border of the Promised Land (Canaan), the Canaanites, who lived there already, were powerful, and their cities were strongly fortified. Then, just as the Israelites were about to cross the border, Moses died. So it was Joshua, Moses' successor, who led the Israelites across the Jordan River near Jericho and into Canaan. The river miraculously dried up, allowing the Israelites to cross – a sign that God was with them. One by one, the great Canaanite cities began to fall before the invading Israelite armies, starting with the mighty city of Jericho. After Joshua's victories, many Canaanites remained in the land, but they could not stop Joshua dividing it between the twelve tribes of Israel. Joshua gave each tribe an area of land, which was further divided between the chief "clans" or groups of the tribe. It was a long and difficult process, but eventually the Israelites peacefully settled in the land that God had promised to Abraham centuries earlier.

THE LAND OF MILK AND HONEY
While the Israelites were wandering in the barren Sinai Desert, Moses described the beauty of the Promised Land that awaited them. He said it was "a land of flowing streams and pools of water...It is a land of wheat and barley, of grapevines, fig trees, pomegranates, olives, and honey. It is a land where food is plentiful and nothing is lacking." When the Israelites finally arrived in Canaan, they discovered this to be true.

Hazor was the most powerful Canaanite city of all. When Joshua captured it, he burned the city to the ground.

SEA OF GALILEE

Hazor

Madon

King Jabin of Hazor ruled over most of Canaan. He was rich and powerful, with a huge army.

Rahab and the spies
Joshua sent two men from the Israelite camp at Shittim to spy on Jericho. While there, they were seen, so they hid in the house of a woman called Rahab, who lived on the city wall. She looked after them because, as she said to them, "I know that God has given this land to you Israelites." Then, when darkness fell, Rahab helped the men to escape by climbing down the city walls.

Rahab lowered the Israelite spies down the city walls on a rope.

All the Israelite tribes sent soldiers for Joshua's campaigns. This included the tribes of Reuben, Gad, and Manasseh, who had already settled east of the Jordan River.

Shimron

Achshaph

Dor

With its huge defensive walls, the city of Jericho was a daunting sight for the Israelites.

MEDITERRANEAN SEA

Far away in the distance, the fertile lands of Canaan lay beyond the Jordan River.

The Jordan River flows into the Dead Sea.

Moses sees the Promised Land
While the Israelites were wandering in the parched Sinai Desert, a spring of water miraculously appeared from a rock. Because Moses pretended that he, and not God, had performed the miracle, God told Moses that he would see the Promised Land but never enter it. Sure enough, when the Israelites were about to cross the Jordan River and enter Canaan, Moses climbed Mount Nebo and God showed him the Promised Land in the distance. Then Moses died, and Joshua took over as leader of the Israelites.

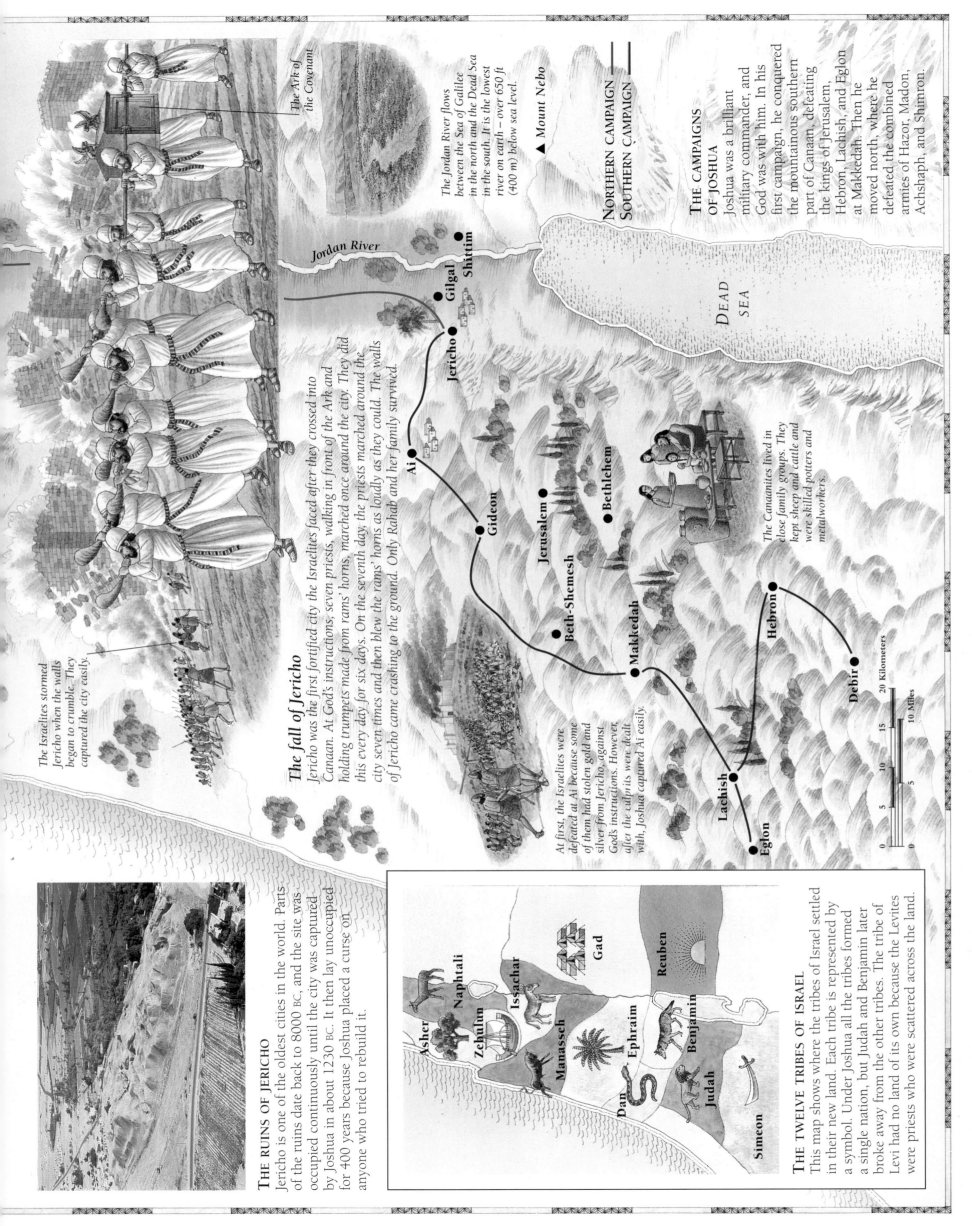

The Ark of the Covenant

The Israelites stormed Jericho when the walls began to crumble. They captured the city easily.

The Jordan River flows between the Sea of Galilee in the north and the Dead Sea in the south. It is the lowest river on earth – over 650 ft (400 m) below sea level.

▲ *Mount Nebo*

NORTHERN CAMPAIGN
SOUTHERN CAMPAIGN

THE CAMPAIGNS OF JOSHUA
Joshua was a brilliant military commander, and God was with him. In his first campaign, he conquered the mountainous southern part of Canaan, defeating the kings of Jerusalem, Hebron, Lachish, and Eglon at Makkedah. Then he moved north, where he defeated the combined armies of Hazor, Madon, Achshaph, and Shimron.

Jordan River

Shittim
Gilgal
Jericho
Ai
Gideon
Jerusalem
Bethlehem
Beth-Shemesh
Makkedah
Hebron
Lachish
Debir
Eglon

DEAD SEA

The Canaanites lived in close family groups. They kept sheep and cattle and were skilled potters and metalworkers.

The fall of Jericho
Jericho was the first fortified city the Israelites faced after they crossed into Canaan. At God's instructions, seven priests, walking in front of the Ark and holding trumpets made from rams' horns, marched once around the city. They did this every day for six days. On the seventh day, the priests marched around the city seven times and then blew the rams' horns as loudly as they could. The walls of Jericho came crashing to the ground. Only Rahab and her family survived.

At first, the Israelites were defeated at Ai because some of them had stolen gold and silver from Jericho, against God's instructions. However, after the culprits were dealt with, Joshua captured Ai easily.

20 Kilometers
15
10
5
0
20 Miles
10
5
0

THE RUINS OF JERICHO
Jericho is one of the oldest cities in the world. Parts of the ruins date back to 8000 BC, and the site was occupied continuously until the city was captured by Joshua in about 1230 BC. It then lay unoccupied for 400 years because Joshua placed a curse on anyone who tried to rebuild it.

THE TWELVE TRIBES OF ISRAEL
This map shows where the tribes of Israel settled in their new land. Each tribe is represented by a symbol. Under Joshua all the tribes formed a single nation, but Judah and Benjamin later broke away from the other tribes. The tribe of Levi had no land of its own because the Levites were priests who were scattered across the land.

Asher
Naphtali
Zebulun
Issachar
Manasseh
Gad
Reuben
Dan
Ephraim
Benjamin
Judah
Simeon

The Philistines' distinctively painted pottery shows that they probably came from Greece and Cyprus, where similar pottery has been found.

Hazor

SEA OF GALILEE

Samson once caught some wild jackals, tied burning torches to their tails, and chased them into the Philistines' fields at harvest time.

Lions roamed the Canaan countryside at this time. Samson once killed a lion with his bare hands.

The Philistines defeated the Israelites on Mount Gilboa, deep in Israelite territory. This is where Saul died.

Samson is betrayed

The greatest of the Israelite judges was Samson, who had enormous strength. On one occasion he escaped from the Philistine city of Gaza by tearing the wooden city gates out of the ground. The Philistines hated him and tried hard to capture him, but he was too strong. Then he fell in love with a beautiful Philistine girl called Delilah, who betrayed him. He told her his deepest secret – that his strength depended on his long hair. While he slept, she cut off his hair, and then called the Philistine soldiers to tie him up. To his horror, Samson found that he could not resist – he had lost his strength.

Delilah held Samson's hair as the guards captured him.

PHILISTINE COFFIN MASK

When they buried their dead, the Philistines made distinctive lids for the coffins, with faces molded into the lid like this one. They may have adopted this custom from Egypt, but sometimes the faces have an upright feather headdress as part of the molding, and this shows them to be Philistines.

The Philistines' chief god was called Dagon. He is usually represented as half fish, half man.

ISRAEL AND THE PHILISTINES

A FEW YEARS AFTER the Israelites settled in the Promised Land more invaders arrived, this time from the sea. The most famous of these "Sea Peoples" – the Philistines – settled in an area that the Israelites had not occupied, south of the territory of Dan, west of the territory of Judah, and centered on the five cities of Ashdod, Ekron, Ashkelon, Gath, and Gaza. For the next six hundred years, the Philistines were enemies of the Israelites. After the Israelite leader Joshua, the Israelites were ruled by a series of "judges." One of the judges, Samson, won many great battles against the Philistines, but eventually the Israelites decided that they needed a king to help them defeat the Philistines. So the last judge, Samuel, anointed Saul as the first king of the Israelites. When Saul disobeyed God, Samuel chose David to be king instead. David had already won a famous victory over the Philistines by killing their hero, Goliath.

Samson destroys the Philistine temple

After capturing Samson, the Philistines cut out his eyes and kept him in prison in Gaza. In prison Samson prayed, and his hair started to grow again. The Philistines held a huge festival to praise their god Dagon for helping them to catch Samson. They led Samson into Dagon's temple, where thousands of people had gathered. Samson prayed, "Lord God, give me strength just one more time!" Then he pushed against the temple pillars with all his might, and the temple came crashing down, killing Samson and the Philistines together.

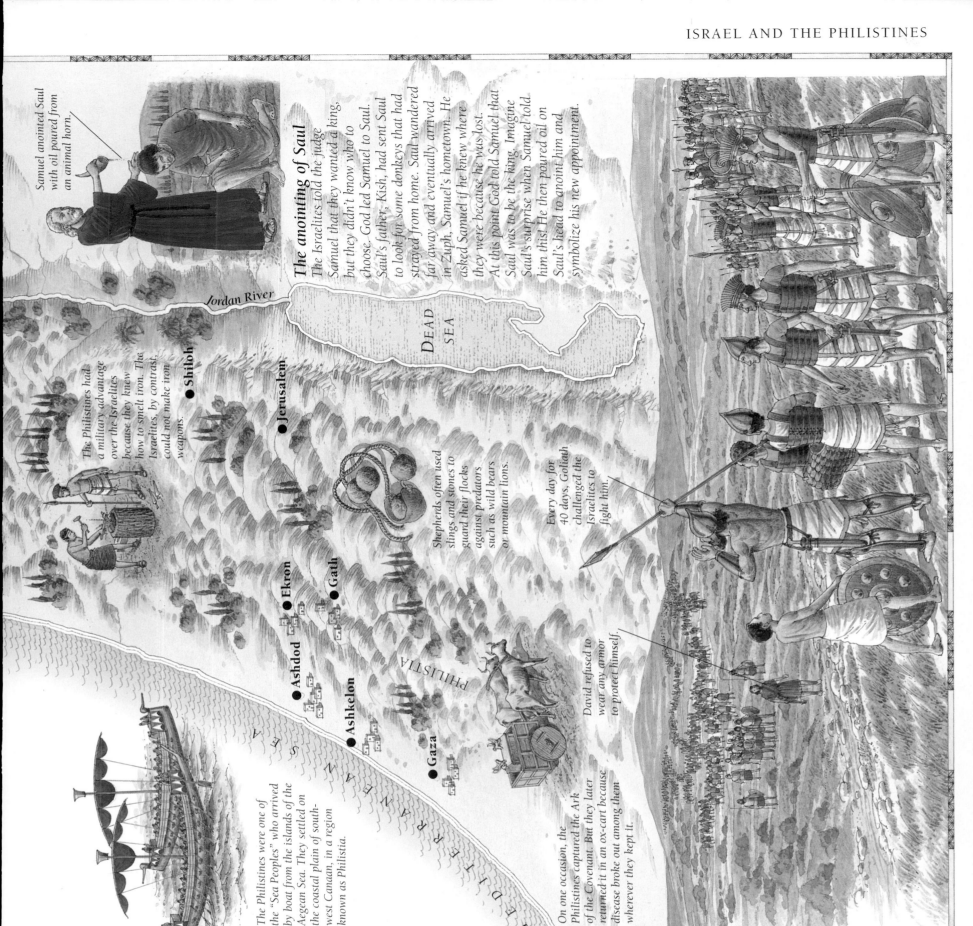

Samuel anointed Saul with oil poured from an animal horn.

The anointing of Saul

The Israelites told the judge Samuel that they wanted a king, but they didn't know who to choose. God led Samuel to Saul. Saul's father, Kish, had sent Saul to look for some donkeys that had strayed from home. Saul wandered far away and eventually arrived in Zuph, Samuel's hometown. He asked Samuel if he knew where they were because he was lost. At this point God told Samuel that Saul was to be the king. Imagine Saul's surprise when Samuel told him this! He then poured oil on Saul's head to anoint him and symbolize his new appointment.

Jordan River

The Philistines had a military advantage over the Israelites because they knew how to smelt iron. The Israelites, by contrast, could not make iron weapons.

DEAD SEA

●Shiloh

●Jerusalem

●Ekron

●Gath

●Ashdod

●Ashkelon

●Gaza

PHILISTIA

Shepherds often used slings and stones to guard their flocks against predators such as wild bears or mountain lions.

Every day for 40 days, Goliath challenged the Israelites to fight him.

David refused to wear any armor to protect himself.

On one occasion, the Philistines captured the Ark of the Covenant. But they later returned it in an ox-cart because disease broke out among them wherever they kept it.

The Philistines were one of the "Sea Peoples" who arrived by boat from the islands of the Aegean Sea. They settled on the coastal plain of south-west Canaan, in a region known as Philistia.

MEDITERRANEAN SEA

PHILISTINES IN HEADDRESSES

The Philistines are often pictured, along with other "Sea Peoples," in the friezes of Egyptian temples. This stone relief from the temple of Rameses III in Thebes shows Philistine soldiers being taken prisoner by Egyptians. We can tell from the frieze that the Philistines were clean-shaven and wore feather headdresses, with feathers rising vertically from a band worn around the forehead. Philistine soldiers carried long spears, round shields, and triangular daggers.

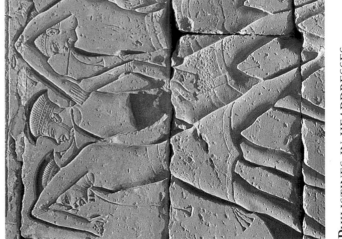

David and Goliath

The Philistines were gaining victories over the Israelites due to a Philistine warrior named Goliath. He was a giant – nearly 8 ft (2.4 m) tall and enormously strong. The whole Israelite army was afraid of him. But a young man named David believed that, with God's help, he could defeat him. He took the sling that he used to scare animals away from his father's sheep, and approached Goliath, who was shouting threats. David shouted back, "How dare you defy the God of the armies of Israel!" Then he fired a stone so hard that it killed Goliath outright.

0 10 20 30 40 Kilometers
0 10 20 Miles

21

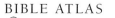

DAVID'S KINGDOM

DAVID STARTED LIFE AS a humble shepherd in Bethlehem, but after his victory over Goliath he became famous. When Saul died, the people of Judah made David their king in Hebron, while Saul's son, Ishbosheth, ruled the northern tribes from Mahanaim. However, Ishbosheth was cruelly murdered, and the other tribes asked David to become their king, too. To show this new unity, David made Jerusalem the new capital city of the whole land. The date was just before 1000 BC. David's power grew rapidly and he led Israel's armies in many great victories over the Philistines. Other fierce neighbors – the Moabites, the Edomites, the Ammonites, and even the Syrians – also submitted to his rule and began paying taxes to Israel. For 40 years David ruled well and God promised him that one of his descendants would always be king in Jerusalem. This is why Jesus is referred to as the "Son of David" – people believed he was the new king the Israelites had been waiting for.

DAVID'S TOWER
Before David became king, Jerusalem was occupied by a Canaanite tribe. David captured the city from them and then built new fortifications all round it to make it a strong capital for the Israelites. The tower in this photograph was built 1,000 years later, by King Herod, on the same site as David's new walls.

The return of the Ark

As soon as he became king, David held a great festival to bring the Ark of the Covenant into Jerusalem. He wanted to thank God for protecting and supporting him. People came from all over the land to join in the celebrations and see the Ark and the special tent that David had made for it. There was dancing and singing, music and feasting, and a huge procession led by David, who danced at the front of the procession as the Ark entered the city. Everyone was delighted with their new king.

The Ark of the Covenant

EGYPT

Nile River

Nile River

David and his music

David was an expert musician. After he killed Goliath, King Saul employed him to play the lyre and sing. Whenever Saul felt sad, David's music would cheer him up. Later, when David himself was king, his songs became famous. David always sang about God and about God's love for his people. These songs are known as "psalms."

MEDIEVAL PSALTER
A "Psalter" is the name for a book containing the Psalms. This beautiful Psalter was made by hand in about 1320, probably for a wealthy merchant to use in his private prayers. The page shows Psalm 101, one of the many psalms written by David.

The Lord is my shepherd

In the much loved psalm 23, David remembers how he cared for his sheep in Bethlehem, and then pictures himself as a sheep in God's flock, being cared for by God himself.

"The Lord is my shepherd; I have everything I need. He lets me rest in green meadows; he leads me beside peaceful streams. He renews my strength. He guides me along right paths, bringing honor to his name." (Psalm 23:1–3)

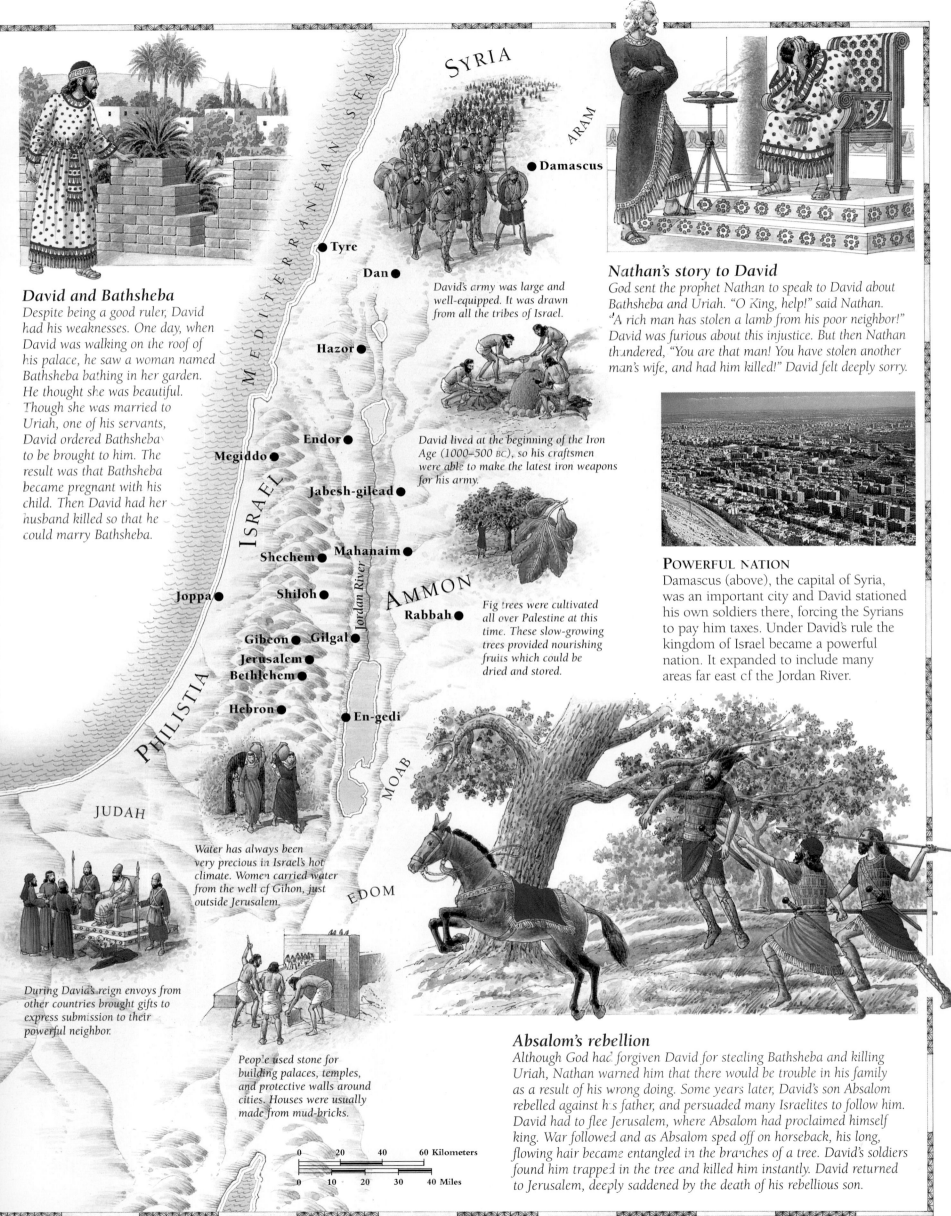

David and Bathsheba

Despite being a good ruler, David had his weaknesses. One day, when David was walking on the roof of his palace, he saw a woman named Bathsheba bathing in her garden. He thought she was beautiful. Though she was married to Uriah, one of his servants, David ordered Bathsheba to be brought to him. The result was that Bathsheba became pregnant with his child. Then David had her husband killed so that he could marry Bathsheba.

David's army was large and well-equipped. It was drawn from all the tribes of Israel.

David lived at the beginning of the Iron Age (1000–500 BC), so his craftsmen were able to make the latest iron weapons for his army.

Fig trees were cultivated all over Palestine at this time. These slow-growing trees provided nourishing fruits which could be dried and stored.

Water has always been very precious in Israel's hot climate. Women carried water from the well of Gihon, just outside Jerusalem.

During David's reign envoys from other countries brought gifts to express submission to their powerful neighbor.

People used stone for building palaces, temples, and protective walls around cities. Houses were usually made from mud-bricks.

Nathan's story to David

God sent the prophet Nathan to speak to David about Bathsheba and Uriah. "O King, help!" said Nathan. "A rich man has stolen a lamb from his poor neighbor!" David was furious about this injustice. But then Nathan thundered, "You are that man! You have stolen another man's wife, and had him killed!" David felt deeply sorry.

POWERFUL NATION

Damascus (above), the capital of Syria, was an important city and David stationed his own soldiers there, forcing the Syrians to pay him taxes. Under David's rule the kingdom of Israel became a powerful nation. It expanded to include many areas far east of the Jordan River.

Absalom's rebellion

Although God had forgiven David for stealing Bathsheba and killing Uriah, Nathan warned him that there would be trouble in his family as a result of his wrong doing. Some years later, David's son Absalom rebelled against his father, and persuaded many Israelites to follow him. David had to flee Jerusalem, where Absalom had proclaimed himself king. War followed and as Absalom sped off on horseback, his long, flowing hair became entangled in the branches of a tree. David's soldiers found him trapped in the tree and killed him instantly. David returned to Jerusalem, deeply saddened by the death of his rebellious son.

Map labels: SYRIA, ARAM, Damascus, MEDITERRANEAN SEA, Tyre, Dan, Hazor, Endor, Megiddo, Jabesh-gilead, ISRAEL, Shechem, Mahanaim, Shiloh, Joppa, AMMON, Rabbah, Jordan River, Gibeon, Gilgal, Jerusalem, Bethlehem, Hebron, En-gedi, MOAB, JUDAH, PHILISTIA, EDOM

0 20 40 60 Kilometers
0 10 20 30 40 Miles

SOLOMON'S TEMPLE

SOLOMON BECAME KING OF ISRAEL when his
father David died in about 970 BC. Because David
had been so successful, Solomon inherited a large kingdom, with taxes pouring
in from many surrounding lands. Solomon became very rich. He built a huge
palace for himself in Jerusalem and had many servants and many wives. He
divided Israel into 12 districts – each district had to provide food for Solomon's
huge household for one month each year. Solomon was also a clever businessman.
He bought horses from Egypt and then sold them to traders from other countries.
Solomon's merchant ships brought gold to Jerusalem, and other exciting imports
from Africa, such as parrots, spices, ivory, and perfume. He married the daughter
of the Egyptian pharaoh and built a palace for her beside his own. However,
Solomon's biggest project was the building of a magnificent temple,
where all the Israelites could come to worship God.

CEDAR TRANSPORTED BY SEA
This Assyrian stone carving shows
ships similar to the ones Solomon
used to bring cedar from Tyre. Hiram,
the king of Tyre, was Solomon's ally,
and provided all the wood and much
of the gold for Solomon's Temple.

KING SOLOMON'S MINES
These rock columns standing
in the desert south of Jerusalem
are called "Solomon's Pillars."
They are named in memory of
the famous mines from which
Solomon obtained precious
metals for his great buildings.
Near these columns are some
ancient copper mines which
Solomon may have worked.

*Copper was obtained by
digging copper ore out of the
ground and then heating it until
the metal melted and collected
at the bottom of the furnace.*

Western Gate

Citadel

Citadel wall

Water Gate

*Long caravans of camels
arrived at Jerusalem,
bringing precious wood
and spices from the East.*

City wall

The Queen of Sheba

*Rumors of Solomon's wealth and wisdom
spread far and wide. The Queen of Sheba
arrived from her distant kingdom, probably
in Ethiopia, in order to meet this famous
king. She asked Solomon all the difficult
questions she could think of, and he
answered them wisely. The queen visited the
Temple and Solomon's palace and throne-
room. She saw his servants and soldiers in
their rich uniforms, and met his many wives
living in luxury. Then she said to Solomon,
"It is all much greater than everything I
heard! Blessed be the Lord your God, who
has delighted in you." Before she left, the
queen gave Solomon many magnificent gifts.*

The city of Jerusalem

Like King David, Solomon continued to extend and strengthen the walls around Jerusalem. The city grew in wealth and beauty. In 1 Kings 10:27 it says "The king made silver as plentiful in Jerusalem as stones." Under the Temple Mount Solomon built huge stables to house the hundreds of horses and chariots in his army.

Temple Mount

Solomon's wisdom

When Solomon became king, he asked God for the gift of wisdom, so that he could rule well. One day, two women came to Solomon to ask him to settle a dispute. The women lived together and both had recently given birth. One of the babies had died, and its mother had swapped her dead baby for the living one and pretended it was hers. Solomon ordered a soldier to divide the live baby in two with a sword, and give each mother half. The guilty mother agreed to this, but the real mother cried, begging Solomon to give the baby to the lying woman rather than kill it. Solomon gave the baby to the mother who cried – he knew that the true mother would not want her baby to be killed.

King David had chosen the location for the Temple before he died. It was built on Mount Moriah, north of the city of Jerusalem, and was believed to be the place where Abraham had nearly sacrificed Isaac.

Palace

Cherubim either side of the Ark

The Holy of Holies – the room in which the Ark of the Covenant was kept.

A chamber called "The Holy Place."

Solomon used many horses, not just for his army, but also to transport building materials to the Temple site.

Boaz

Altar

Storerooms

Jakin

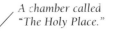

Solomon's Temple

It took Solomon seven years and thousands of slaves to build his magnificent Temple. In front of it stood two huge pillars made of bronze. Solomon called them Jakin and Boaz, which mean "secure" and "strong." Inside, cedar paneling decorated with gold flowers covered the walls. In the inner sanctuary huge cherubims (winged angels) overshadowed the Ark. Outside, there were storerooms where all the golden lamps, pans, and dishes used by the priests were kept. In the courtyard stood a huge bronze "sea" full of water, which was used for various purification rituals. Sacrifices were offered morning and evening at the great altar.

The "sea"

THE DIVIDED KINGDOM AND FOREIGN INVASION

WHEN SOLOMON DIED, his son Rehoboam became the new king of Israel. Sadly, the peace that Israel had enjoyed under Solomon soon came to an end. Rehoboam treated the people very badly, and as a result, ten of the tribes of Israel broke away from him and began to follow a different king named Jeroboam. As a result, the kingdom divided into two: Israel in the north, led by Jeroboam, and Judah in the south, led by Rehoboam. The northern tribes of the divided kingdom were now cut off from the holy city of Jerusalem, and began to worship pagan gods instead of the Lord. God sent prophets, like Elijah, to warn the Israelites of punishment for their failure to love and worship him.

Because the kingdom was divided, it was also very weak. Just seven years after the split, the Egyptian pharaoh Shishak I invaded Judah, taking all the gold and treasures which Solomon had collected. The worst was yet to come. In 724 BC a huge Assyrian army invaded the northern kingdom. Terrible suffering followed and many people were either killed or taken as prisoners to Assyria.

King Ahaz
The tribes of Judah lived in fear of the Assyrians. King Ahaz, one of the southern kings, nailed the Temple doors shut and told the people to worship the gods of Damascus rather than the true God. Ahaz thought that the gods of Damascus might save them from the Assyrians.

JEZEBEL AT THE WINDOW
This ivory carving from Nimrud, in Assyria, may show the face of Jezebel, the wife of Ahab, one of the northern kings. When Israel split into two, the northern kingdom abandoned God, and began to worship Jezebel's god, Baal.

Prophets of Baal
In order to bring the people of Israel back to God, Elijah the prophet arranged a contest. He called all the Israelites to the top of Mount Carmel, where he challenged the prophets of Baal. Elijah told them to ask their god to make fire fall from heaven onto an altar. Of course, they failed. When Elijah prayed to the true God, a massive bolt of lightning crashed down and set fire to the altar built by Elijah. The Israelites were amazed by God's power, and returned to worshiping him.

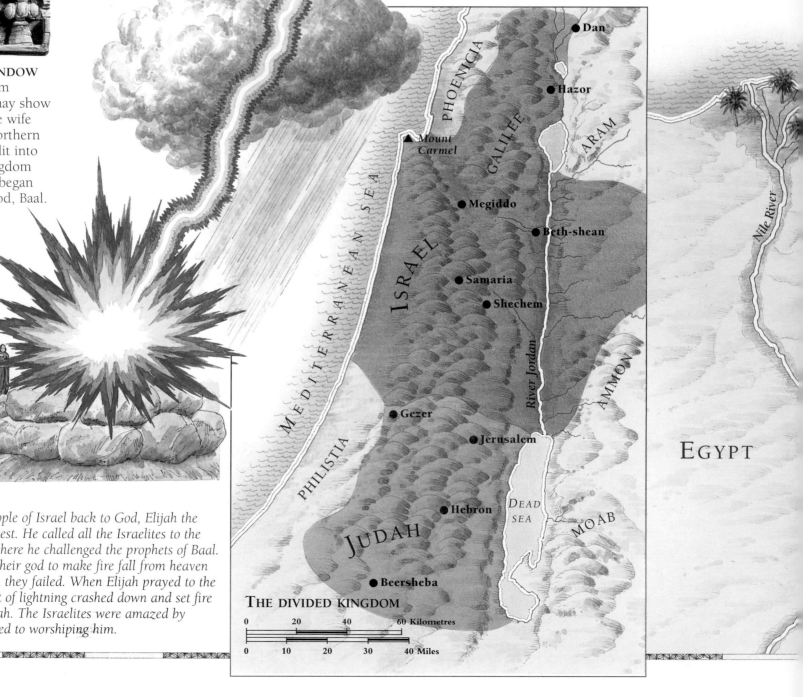

THE DIVIDED KINGDOM

0   20   40   60 Kilometres

0 10 20 30 40 Miles

The power of the Assyrians was so great that all the neighboring kingdoms, including Israel and Judah, had to pay them large amounts of money. These were known as "tributes." If a kingdom refused, the army would take the tribute by force.

Jonah and the big fish

God asked Jonah the prophet to go to Nineveh, the capital of the mighty Assyrian Empire, to warn the people there that they would be punished unless they changed their wicked ways. Jonah refused and ran away to sea – he wanted God to punish the people who had done so much harm to the Israelites. During a terrible storm, God sent a huge fish to swallow Jonah after he was thrown overboard. Inside the fish Jonah prayed, and the Lord commanded the fish to spit him out onto dry land. God asked Jonah to preach to the people of Nineveh a second time. This time, Jonah obeyed.

Nineveh
Nimrud

Euphrates River

Tigris River

Everyone feared the Assyrian armies – their soldiers were well-armed and fought fiercely.

Many trading boats brought rich goods to the Assyrians, just as they once did for Solomon.

Sidon

Tyre

Damascus

ISRAEL

Jerusalem

JUDAH

The Israelites were not allowed to make statues of the Lord, but other peoples often kept statues of their favorite gods in their homes.

Babylon

WALLS AT NINEVEH
In the eighth century BC, Nineveh was the biggest city in the world, with possibly over 100,000 inhabitants. It stood next to the Tigris River and its strong walls stretched for 7.5 miles (12 km) around the city. The Assyrian army would march out through the city gates on campaigns to conquer other nations.

ARABIAN DESERT

THE ASSYRIAN EMPIRE

The palace rooms at Nimrud were very luxurious, with magnificent wall-carvings and paintings. Nimrud was the second city of the Assyrians, after Nineveh, the capital.

PERSIAN GULF

RED SEA

Ivory was skillfully carved to decorate the palaces and temples in Nineveh.

Thebes

The fall of Israel

God became angry with the people of Israel. They had worshiped idols (carved images of gods) and sacrificed children to false gods. Their punishment arrived in the form of a huge Assyrian army, led by King Shalmaneser. In 721 BC, the Assyrians captured the capital city, Samaria. The northern kingdom of Israel ceased to exist. The people of this land were taken as prisoners and scattered to live in various towns in Assyria, while people from Assyria settled in Israel. But when the new Assyrian settlers refused to worship God, he sent fierce lions to attack them.

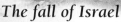

0	100	200	300 Kilometers
0	50	100	150	200 Miles

BABYLON

THE CITY OF BABYLON was a splendid sight. The towering temple of the god Marduk and the magnificent royal palace were among the most impressive buildings in the ancient world. Babylon owed its wealth to its excellent trading position on the banks of the Euphrates River. The city grew especially powerful under King Nebuchadnezzar II, who reigned from 604 to 562 BC. The new king strengthened the city walls, making them wide enough for a four-horse chariot to ride along the top, and constructed the famous Processional Way through the city. It was during this period that Babylon became important in the story of the Jews. Nebuchadnezzar conquered Jerusalem, and many of its inhabitants were forced into exile in Babylon. Among the thousands deported was Ezekiel, who God called to be his prophet during one of Israel's darkest times. The prophet Jeremiah spoke God's truth to those who remained in Judah. The book of Daniel describes this time of exile. It covers the life of the prophet Daniel, the reigns of Nebuchadnezzar II and Belshazzar, and Babylon's fall to the Medes and Persians.

The wise men of Babylon were well trained in astronomy. They studied the planets and stars to predict the future.

THE BABYLONIAN WORLD
This ancient clay tablet is the only surviving Babylonian world map. It shows how the Babylonian mathematicians and astrologers saw the world. Their known world is shown as a circle with the "salt sea" around the edge. Babylon is marked at the center of the map.

Babylon

Aleppo

Ebla

Damascus

Tyre

Jerusalem

DEAD SEA

MEDITERRANEAN SEA

Jerusalem's inhabitants were led into exile by their Babylonian captors.

The fall of Jerusalem
The second book of Kings tells how, in 598 BC, King Nebuchadnezzar II of Babylon besieged Jerusalem with a large army. Eventually the Jews surrendered, and Nebuchadnezzar's soldiers seized the treasures from the Temple and the royal palace. Many Jews were taken captive and forced to march all the way to Babylon. Nebuchadnezzar appointed Jehoiachin's uncle Zedekiah to rule Jerusalem, but after a few years Zedekiah rebelled. Nebuchadnezzar returned to Jerusalem to besiege the city again. After two years Zedekiah and his people were starving to death, but when they tried to escape, the Babylonians captured them, and destroyed the city. Zedekiah was blinded and dragged off to Babylon with the rest of the Jews.

The fiery furnace
Among the exiled Jews in Babylon were three friends – Shadrach, Meshach, and Abednego – who refused to worship the golden statue of Nebuchadnezzar. As punishment, the king threw them into a blazing furnace. To his amazement, the men walked about unharmed by the flames, accompanied by an angel. At once the king released the men and allowed them to worship God as they wished.

The writing on the wall

King Belshazzar, a descendant of Nebuchadnezzar, held a lavish banquet in the royal palace in Babylon. During the feast, the guests drank from golden cups stolen from the temple in Jerusalem. Suddenly a mysterious hand appeared and wrote a strange message on the wall. Belshazzar and his wise men were shocked – they could not understand it. The queen told Belshazzar to call for the Jewish exile Daniel, who had interpreted Nebuchadnezzar's dreams. Daniel explained that because Belshazzar did not honor God, God would divide his kingdom between the Medes and Persians.

Metal workers made objects from gold, copper, and bronze. They cast bronze items by pouring hot, molten metal into open molds.

● **Nineveh**

Tigris River

Euphrates River

The Babylonians wrote on clay tablets, which they stored in "tablet houses."

Leather workers used animal skins to make bags, bottles, harnesses, shoes, and even small boats.

THE TOWER OF BABEL

This painting of the Tower of Babel is by the Flemish painter Pieter Bruegel. The book of Genesis tells how God saw the people of Babel trying to build a tower tall enough to reach the heavens. God destroyed the tower and scattered the people around the world. The Tower of Babel was probably similar in style to the huge temples, or ziggurats, that the Babylonians built to worship their gods.

The largest of the city's entrances was the Ishtar Gate, named after the Babylonian goddess of war. It opened on to the Processional Way, a magnificent route through the center of the city, built by Nebuchadnezzar.

BABYLONIAN EMPIRE

● **Babylon**

● **Nippur**

● **Lagash**

● **Uruk**

Ur ●

The beautiful Hanging Gardens were one of the seven wonders of the ancient world. It is thought that they were built on a series of stepped terraces. Streams, used to water the plants, trickled from top to bottom.

Nebuchadnezzar built a colossal golden statue of himself on the open plain of Dura, near Babylon.

PERSIAN GULF

```
0    50    100    150    200 Kilometers
0         50          100 Miles
```

Daniel in the lions' den

After Babylon's fall to the Medes, King Darius the Mede made Daniel the city's chief administrator. The other administrators were jealous and plotted against Daniel. They persuaded Darius to make a new law, forbidding people to pray to anyone except the king – anyone who refused would be fed to the lions. When the officials caught Daniel praying to God, Darius reluctantly sent Daniel into the lions' den. However, God sent an angel to close the lions' mouths and Daniel's life was spared.

ISHTAR LION

This lion was set into the walls that lined Babylon's great Processional Way. The lion was the symbol of Ishtar, the goddess of fertility and war. She was one of the most important of the city's many gods and goddesses.

THE PERSIAN EMPIRE

KING CYRUS
This marble head could be Cyrus the Great himself, or one of the other great Persian kings, such as his son, Cambyses. Cyrus was famous for his tolerance of non-Persian religions and gods.

THE PERSIAN EMPIRE was very large. For 200, years its rule stretched from Greece to India, and from Egypt to Uzbekistan. The empire began in 550 BC, when a young Persian king named Cyrus captured Ecbatana, the capital of the kingdom of Media. Cyrus then marched west and captured Lydia. As his power grew he became bolder, and finally, in 539 BC, he captured Babylon, the greatest city in the world. Cyrus then settled in Susa, his new capital. He divided his empire into 127 provinces, and established an empire-wide postal system so that the messages could travel quickly across this vast empire. Cyrus decided that all the Israelites whom the Babylonians had captured and kept in Babylon should be allowed to return home. So, with great joy, the Israelites made the long journey home on foot – about 1,056 miles (1,700 km) – their carts piled high with their belongings.

To speed up their postal system, the Persians built the famous Royal Road. It stretched from Sardis to Susa – about 1,554 miles (2,500 km) long.

BLACK SEA

THRACE

MACEDONIA

LYDIA

• Athens

• Sardis

• Ephesus

CARIA

CILICIA

MEDITERRANEAN SEA

ABAR NAHARA

• Damascus

LIBYA

• Jerusalem

• Memphis

SINAI

ARABIA

Nile River

EGYPT

RED SEA

In 525 BC, the Persians added Egypt to their empire. Although the Egyptians were defeated, the Persians always feared that they might rebel.

The Temple is rebuilt
King Cyrus allowed the Jews to bring back to Jerusalem all the gold and silver treasures that the Babylonians had taken from the Temple. But now, there was no Temple to put them in – sadly, it had been destroyed by the Babylonians 50 years before. So, encouraged by the prophets Haggai and Zechariah, the people laid new foundations, and everyone was overjoyed. The people who remembered the glory of the old Temple wept when they saw the work beginning on the new, more humble Temple.

ROYAL ROAD ———

| 0 | 100 | 200 | 300 | 400 Kilometers |

| 0 | 100 | 200 | 300 Miles |

Ezra and the Book of the Law
It took many years to rebuild Jerusalem after being so badly damaged by the Babylonians. Once the Temple and the city walls were finished, all the Israelites came to Jerusalem for a great celebration. Ezra, one of their leaders, stood on a special wooden platform and read from the Bible, the Book of the Law that God had given his people. The Israelites were filled with joy and worshiped God with all their hearts. After the reading, there was a great celebration with songs of thanksgiving.

Rebuilding the walls

Though people were living in Jerusalem again, the Persians would not permit the Israelites to build new city walls. They were afraid that if it was fortified, the Egyptians might use Jerusalem as a base for rebellion. Finally, in 444 BC, King Artaxerxes allowed his trusted servant Nehemiah, who was a Jew, to return to Jerusalem and build new walls and gates.

GRAND PALACE AT PERSEPOLIS

Susa was the capital of the Persian Empire, but the Persian kings built magnificent new palaces at Persepolis, in Iran. Here the kings sat in huge throne rooms, where musicians entertained them, great banquets were held, and gifts were brought to them from foreign kings.

Camels were ideal for long distance travel. However, they were expensive and only the wealthy could afford to travel this way.

Persian kings had their own special soldiers called "the immortals."

Esther's banquet

Life was hard for the Jews in the Persian Empire. Haman, the Persian prime minister, hated the Jews and persuaded King Ahasuerus to kill them all. However, Esther, the king's beautiful wife, was a Jew. She invited the king and Haman to a banquet and denounced Haman's cruel plot. Then, Haman had to beg for his own life.

From all over the empire, gold and silver poured into Susa and Persepolis. This was tribute, or payment, from conquered lands.

The first Jewish exiles returned to Jerusalem in 538 BC. Their journey was long and hard, but also joyful, because they were able to return to their homelands.

ALEXANDER THE GREAT

Alexander was one of the fiercest and most intelligent Greek commanders of all time. In 334 BC, he set out from Macedonia with his army and defeated the Persians in Lydia. The Persian king, Darius, quickly led a huge army from Susa, and a fierce battle took place at Issos. However, Darius lost, and Alexander captured all the Persian gold in the treasury at Damascus. He then marched south to conquer both Jerusalem and Egypt. Within three years the whole empire was Alexander's. The Persian Empire had ended and the Greek Empire had begun.

31

THE NEW TESTAMENT

THE 27 BOOKS OF THE NEW TESTAMENT describe the life, death, and resurrection of Jesus Christ and the birth of the early church. Much of Jesus' life was spent in the towns and fishing villages along the shores of the Sea of Galilee. Here, in the northernmost region of Palestine, he performed miracles and taught people about God. The dramatic events leading up to Jesus' crucifixion took place further south in Jerusalem – the bustling center of Jewish life. After Jesus' death and resurrection, Paul began his famous missionary journeys. Most of the events of the New Testament then occurred beyond the Holy Land. Paul traveled far, taking the message of Christianity to Asia Minor and Greece before making the perilous sea journey to Rome itself.

Jesus enters Jerusalem
As Jesus rode into Jerusalem on a donkey, his followers waved palm branches and threw their coats down in his path. "Jesus is King!" they cried.

The Sea of Galilee

JESUS' BIRTH AND EARLY LIFE

FIVE HUNDRED YEARS had passed since the Jews had been allowed to return to Jerusalem. But they were still not free. In the first century BC, the Holy Land (or Palestine) became part of the vast Roman Empire. The Jews had their own king, Herod, but he only ruled with the permission of the Roman emperor Augustus, who was over 1,200 miles (2,000 km) away in Rome. When Augustus wanted to know how much tax he could demand from Herod's kingdom he ordered everybody to return to their family homes to be registered. This is when the story of Jesus begins. A young woman called Mary had heard from the angel Gabriel that she was to be the mother of God's son. Just before the baby was due, Mary and her husband Joseph traveled 75 miles (120 km) from Nazareth in Galilee to Joseph's family home in Bethlehem to be registered. On the night they arrived in Bethlehem, Mary gave birth to a son, the baby Jesus.

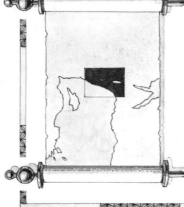

The angel Gabriel visits Mary

Mary had just become engaged to Joseph, a young carpenter from Nazareth. One day, a glowing angel suddenly appeared before her. Mary was terrified, but the angel told her not to be afraid. "You are special! You have been chosen by God to be the mother of his son," the angel Gabriel said. "But I'm not yet married," Mary replied. "How can I have a baby?" The angel told her that God's power would make it happen, and that the child would be the Son of God himself. The baby was to be called Jesus, which means "Savior." Mary was amazed at what she had heard, but she said, "I will accept whatever God wants."

Roman soldiers on the march were a common sight in Palestine. Herod ruled only by permission of the Romans, who kept an army in Jerusalem.

Many Roman officials worked for Herod. Some of them were involved in collecting taxes, which Herod had to pay to the Romans.

Many people made a living as fishermen on the Sea of Galilee. Nets constantly needed mending, and fishermen would spend many hours reknitting them.

Jesus probably helped Joseph in his carpentry workshop. Here they most likely made plows, carts, doors, and household tools for the people of Nazareth.

• **Sidon**

• **Tyre**

SEA OF GALILEE

• **Sepphoris** • **Nazareth**

GALILEE

• **Scythopolis**

• **Pella**

• **Dor**

• **Caesarea**

The birth of Jesus

Bethlehem was crowded with people who had traveled there for the census. Mary and Joseph searched for a room in which to spend the night, but all the inns were full. The only place they found to stay was a stable. That night, Jesus was born. Mary wrapped him in strips of cloth and laid him in a manger to keep him warm. In the fields above Bethlehem a group of angels told some shepherds about the birth of a Savior. The shepherds hurried down from the hills to worship the baby Jesus.

Herod meets the wise men

Everyone in Jerusalem was talking about the arrival of some strange men dressed in rich eastern clothes, who were following a bright star in the night sky. King Herod summoned them. "You say that the star means the birth of a new king?" he asked. "Yes," they replied. "He was born in Bethlehem." Herod began to plot the death of the new king. He asked the wise men to tell him exactly where this king lived. But after visiting Jesus, they returned home by a different route because God warned them in a dream not to return to Herod.

AUGUSTUS CAESAR

The name "Augustus," which means "glorious," was given to Gaius Julius Caesar Octavianus, the first Roman emperor, in 27 BC. During the reign of Augustus, the Roman Empire almost reached its greatest extent, with 36 provinces stretching from Spain in the west to Judea and Syria in the east. Augustus was still ruling the Roman Empire when Jesus was born, in about 5 BC.

The boy Jesus in the Temple

We know very little about Jesus' childhood. But Luke's Gospel tells us that when Jesus was 12 years old, Mary and Joseph took him with them to Jerusalem for the annual Passover celebrations. Jesus was fascinated by the Temple and forgot the time as he listened and talked to the famous Jewish teachers there. The religious leaders were astonished at the breadth of his knowledge. He stayed there after the Passover had ended. On their way back to Nazareth, Mary and Joseph suddenly realized that Jesus was missing. They spent three anxious days hunting all over Jerusalem for him. When at last they found him in the Temple, Jesus said, "Why were you worried? Didn't you know that I would be in my Father's house?"

Jordan River

●Jericho

Machaerus ●

DEAD SEA

SAMARIA

●Jerusalem
●Bethlehem
●Herodium

JUDEA

Masada ●

Herod started to build a magnificent new temple in Jerusalem in 19 BC. It was destroyed by the Romans in AD 70, but its foundations still stand.

●Ascalon

●Gaza

The Herodium, just 3 miles (5 km) from Bethlehem, was Herod's favorite fortress. Herod was buried here in 4 BC, after a long procession brought his body from Jericho, the city in which he had died.

0   10   20   30   40 Kilometers
0   10   20 Miles

MASADA

King Herod built many powerful fortresses, and Masada was the greatest outside Jerusalem. It was built on a steep, flat-topped hill near the Dead Sea. When the Romans later fought the Jews, Masada was the last Jewish fortress to fall (in AD 73). In order to gain access to the top, the Romans had to build a massive ramp, which you can see on the right in this picture.

JESUS BEGINS HIS MINISTRY

JESUS GREW UP IN NAZARETH, a small village in the hills of southern Galilee. He worked peacefully as a carpenter, helping his father Joseph. However, things were not so peaceful elsewhere. The Romans ruled the country, and feelings toward them were mixed in the Jewish community. Some of the Jews, like Herod Antipas, the governor of Galilee, liked Roman rule because it was the Romans who kept them in power. Others, such as the Pharisees, resented the Romans and longed for God to save Israel from them. Some terrorist groups had even attacked Roman soldiers, especially in Judea and Jerusalem where the Roman forces were strongest. In this confused and dangerous situation, Jesus began to preach and minister to the troubled people. When he was 30 years old, Jesus was baptized in the Jordan by his cousin John, marking the beginning of his amazing ministry. He started to travel around Galilee with his chosen followers, known as the disciples, teaching in the synagogues, preaching on hillsides and beside the Sea of Galilee. Jesus knew that God the Father was working through him.

GALILEE
Jesus grew up in a region called Galilee, west of the Sea of Galilee. In the northern part of the region are high mountains. In Jesus' time, most people lived to the south – in the villages along the shore of the lake or in the rolling hills behind. Galilee was a Roman province, and was ruled by Herod Antipas, from his palace in Tiberias.

Temptations in the wilderness
After Jesus was baptized, God's Spirit sent him alone into the desert. There, for forty days, Jesus fasted and prayed to the Lord. During these forty days, the devil visited Jesus and tried to persuade him to sin. However, Jesus resisted the devil's temptations, and obeyed God the Father.

Stones into bread
The devil tried to tempt Jesus to turn stones into bread. Although he was hungry, Jesus refused to use God's power for himself. He knew that he must rely entirely on God to meet his needs.

Falling from the temple
Next, the devil asked Jesus to jump off the high point of a temple. The devil said that as the Son of God, Jesus would be protected by angels. Jesus again refused – he would not test God's power.

Kingdoms of the world
"You can have all this, if you worship me!" said the devil, showing Jesus the whole world from the top of a mountain. "No!" replied Jesus. "You must worship the Lord your God; serve him alone." After this final temptation, the devil disappeared and angels appeared to tend to Jesus.

John baptizes Jesus
Huge crowds flocked from Jerusalem, Judea, and Galilee to hear the teachings of John the Baptist. They were excited, wondering whether John could be the Messiah – the "special Savior" – they were expecting. As he saw Jesus coming towards him, John exclaimed, "Look, the Lamb of God, who takes away the sin of the world!" Then, after John had baptized Jesus, a miraculous thing happened. God's Holy Spirit came down in the form of a dove and settled on Jesus. God publicly showed that Jesus was the Messiah and he spoke his approval from heaven.

MEDITERRANEAN SEA

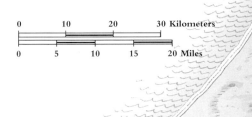

0	10	20	30 Kilometers
0	5	10	15	20 Miles

On every Sabbath day (Saturday) Jews would gather for worship in their synagogues. Many synagogues were also used as schools.

Sidon

Tyre

Caesarea
Philippi

SYRIA

Mount Hermon towers 9,124 ft
(2,774 m) in the north of Israel.
Here, the Jordan River begins its
long journey to the Dead Sea. It is
believed that Jesus revealed himself
as the Son of God (known as the
Transfiguraton) on Mount Hermon.

Traditional country houses in Galilee
were made of mud-brick and had flat
roofs. Crops, such as grapes, would
often be dried on the roofs.

Capernaum

Cana

Magdala
Tiberias

Sepphoris

Nazareth

SEA OF
GALILEE

GALILEE

TETRARCHY OF PHILIP

Nain

Jordan River

DECAPOLIS

SAMARIA

Sychar

▲ Mount Gerizim

PERAEA

JUDEA

Jericho

Bethabara

Jerusalem

Bethlehem

WILDERNESS OF JUDEA

DEAD
SEA

Machaerus

Machaerus was the site of Herod Antipas'
favorite fortress. This is where John the
Baptist was beheaded by Herod's soldiers.

The Transfiguration

When Jesus visited Caesarea Philippi, he began to question his disciples.
"Who do people say I am?" Jesus asked them. Peter rightly answered that Jesus
was the Messiah, the son of the living God. Six days later, Jesus took three of his
disciples, Peter, James, and John, up to a mountain to pray. Suddenly, he began
to glow brightly with God's glory. Moses and Elijah appeared beside Jesus, and
spoke with him. The three disciples fell to the ground in fear. A beautiful bright
cloud appeared, from which God's voice was heard to say: "This is my Son,
whom I love. Listen to him!" Jesus calmly told his friends not to be afraid.

The Pharisees were
the leading teachers
of the Torah (Jewish
law and teaching).
They were highly
respected, and devoted
their lives to studying.

The wedding at Cana

One day Jesus and his mother Mary were invited to a wedding at Cana, in
Galilee. In the middle of the party, Mary noticed that the wine had run out,
so she asked Jesus to help. Jesus quietly told the waiting staff to fill six stone
jars with water, and to serve it to the guests of the banquet. Reluctantly they
agreed, but as they poured it into the guest's cups, they found that the water
had miraculously turned into wine. People were amazed when the servants
revealed what Jesus had done. This was Jesus' first miracle.

Women in Galilee worked
hard. It was their duty to
keep the home clean and
prepare all the family's
meals. They also worked
in the fields at harvest time.

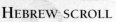
The Torah scroll is kept
safe in an ivory casing.

The text is written
on a scroll made of
parchment paper.

HEBREW SCROLL

Jewish life centers around obedience to God's
law contained in the first five books of the
Bible, known as the Torah, which means
"teaching." The texts are copied down in
Hebrew, and sections are read out at Jewish
services in synagogues. Jesus read from the
scroll of Isaiah upon his return to Nazareth.

THE MIRACLES OF JESUS

WHEN JESUS TURNED WATER into wine at the wedding in Cana, it was the start of a remarkable series of miracles. In particular, Jesus had wonderful healing power – he could heal people of any disease just by touching them and commanding the sickness to leave. People from all over Galilee came to find him, bringing their sick relatives and friends. As Jesus' reputation spread, people came from even further away – from Syria in the north, from Judea in the south, or from the Decapolis, the region east of the Sea of Galilee. Jesus traveled too, moving from town to town in Galilee with his disciples. Wherever he went he spoke about God's kingdom. He told people that his miracles were a sign of God's kingdom arriving among them. He encouraged people to turn to God with new faith, repenting of their sins. Because of these miracles, many Jews wondered if Jesus was the Messiah (the chosen deliverer of Israel) they had been waiting for to save them from the Romans. However, instead of using his power to deliver Israel from the Romans, Jesus used it to heal the sick, and to reveal the power of God.

MEDITERRANEAN SEA

SYNAGOGUE AT CAPERNAUM
This synagogue at Capernaum was probably built around AD 385, on the site of the earlier synagogue where Jesus taught and healed people. The first synagogue had been built by a wealthy Roman soldier. Here, Jesus uttered these words, "I am the bread of life! Whoever comes to me will never be hungry."

● Ptolemais

The women of the household baked the daily bread. The dough was mixed on a flat stone, allowed to rise, and then baked over an open fire.

Feeding the five thousand
Many people followed Jesus and wanted to hear his teachings. One day, Jesus crossed by boat to the eastern shore of Galilee, hoping to rest with his disciples. But a huge crowd had followed him by walking around the northern end of the lake. Jesus taught them all day. By evening, everyone was hungry, and there was nowhere to buy food. Jesus' disciples were concerned that he should rest, but rather than send the crowds away, Jesus performed a great miracle. A small boy gave five loaves of bread and two small fish to Jesus. After he blessed them, Jesus thanked God for the meal and asked the disciples to pass around the pieces of bread and fish, which had miraculously multiplied. There was enough food to feed every one of the more than five thousand visitors gathered there.

DISCIPLES OF JESUS
Soon after he began his ministry, Jesus chose 12 of his followers to be special disciples and his closest friends. Before he chose them, Jesus had spent a whole night in prayer. The chosen disciples were Simon Peter, Andrew, James, John, Philip, Bartholomew, Thomas, Matthew the tax collector, James, Thaddaeus, Simon the Zealot, and Judas Iscariot. They lived, worked, and traveled with Jesus and witnessed his teaching. After his death and resurrection, they became the twelve apostles (meaning "sent ones"), the founders and leaders of the Christian church. This 19th century painting by artist Adam Brenner shows Jesus calling Simon Peter, Andrew, James, and John. They were the first disciples Jesus called to follow him. He was walking by the Sea of Galilee when he saw Simon Peter and Andrew fishing, and asked them to become "fishers of people."

Jesus heals the paralyzed man

*One day, in Capernaum, Jesus was teaching in a house packed
with people who had come to hear him. Four friends arrived
carrying a paralyzed man. They wanted Jesus to heal him,
but could not make their way through the crowds into the
house. So they climbed onto the flat roof, stripped away
the baked-earth covering and lowered their friend
down through the hole, right in front of Jesus.
"Son," said Jesus, "your sins are forgiven."
And then Jesus healed the man's paralysis.
People were amazed when the man
walked out, carrying his stretcher.*

*Leprosy was a common disease in the time of Jesus.
People with leprosy had to live in a separate
community and wear torn clothing to show that they
were sufferers. Jesus cured a leper in Capernaum.*

THE MOUNT OF BEATITUDES

This church was built on a hillside overlooking the
Sea of Galilee, on the site where Jesus is thought to
have given his famous Beatitudes, or blessings. These
blessings are recorded in Matthew's Gospel, chapter 5.
There are nine blessings – beginning with "Blessed are
the poor in spirit, for theirs is the kingdom of heaven."
Jesus often encouraged those who were poor and weak,
telling them that God would bless them.

● **Bethsaida**

Capernaum ●

▲ *Mount of Beatitudes*

Gennesaret ●

● **Cana**

Magdala ●

*SEA OF
GALILEE*

Tiberias ●

● **Nazareth**

Jordan River

Calming the storm

*Jesus and his disciples were crossing the Sea of Galilee one day
when a huge storm blew up. Jesus was asleep, resting his head
on a cushion in the stern, while Peter and the others desperately
bailed water out of the boat. Eventually they woke him.
"Teacher, help us!" they said. "We're sinking!" Jesus stood up
and spoke to the wind and water in a loud voice: "Peace! Be
still!" The storm died down, and the disciples were amazed.
"Why were you afraid?" Jesus asked them. "Have you no faith?"
The disciples were in awe – even the winds obeyed his word.*

*Galilee was a wealthy
area because traders
from the east passed
through, sometimes
bringing silk or
spices for Rome.*

Jairus' daughter

*In one of the towns by the Sea of Galilee, the leader of the
synagogue had a 12-year-old daughter. One day she fell
seriously ill. Jairus, her father, rushed to find Jesus. "Please,
come before she dies!" he begged. But on their way a messenger
arrived to say that the young girl had died. "Don't be afraid!"
Jesus said to Jairus. "Just have faith." When they reached
Jairus' house, Jesus went in with Peter, James, and John,
as well as Jairus and his wife, and took the girl by the
hand. Gently he raised her to life again, and told her
parents to give her something to eat.*

0 2 4 6 8 Kilometers

0 2 4 6 Miles

JESUS TRAVELS TO JERUSALEM

JESUS SPENT MOST OF HIS MINISTRY in Galilee, but he occasionally traveled south to Jerusalem. All Jews were required to attend the great Jerusalem festivals as often as they could – especially Passover (in April every year), the festival of Weeks (or "Pentecost," in June), and the festival of Tabernacles (in September). John's Gospel describes some of Jesus' festival visits. It was here that Jesus became increasingly unpopular with religious leaders. On one visit he offended some people by healing a man on the Sabbath – a day when Jews are not supposed to work. On another visit Jesus called himself the "light of the world," which deeply offended some of the Pharisees. They felt that Jesus was deceiving people with this bold claim. As the third Passover of his ministry drew near, Jesus knew that his enemies in Jerusalem were plotting to kill him. By now, news of Jesus' amazing ministry had spread far and wide. Luke tells us that on this final journey to Jerusalem, Jesus traveled slowly, stopping often to teach and to heal people. Jesus took a long route, first into Samaria, possibly to Ginae, and then down through the Jordan valley to Jericho. On the way, he told his disciples that he knew he would be tortured and put to death in Jerusalem.

THE PARABLES OF JESUS

In his teaching, Jesus often used scenes and situations from the surrounding countryside that people were familiar with. For instance, he compared God to a shepherd who had lost a sheep and longed to find it, in order to explain how God cares for each and every person. He spoke of the gospel as seeds thrown by a sower into the hearts and minds of people. These picture-stories are called parables.

The Good Samaritan

One day a Jewish lawyer asked Jesus who his neighbor was. In reply, Jesus told the tale of a man who had been mugged and robbed, and left for dead beside the road. Both a priest and a Levite passed by the injured man without stopping to help him. But then a Samaritan stopped and cared for him. Jews and Samaritans were normally great enemies, so Jesus used this story to tell the lawyer we should show love to all people – even those we do not like and to treat them as the good Samaritan did.

MEDITERRANEAN SEA

Shepherds and their flocks did not stay in one place. They traveled around the countryside, looking for good grazing.

JESUS' FINAL JOURNEY TO JERUSALEM ——————

0   5   10   15   20 Kilometers

0   5   10   15 Miles

Zacchaeus the tax collector

In Jericho, huge crowds waited for Jesus to pass by on his journey. The local tax collector was a wealthy, but much hated, man called Zacchaeus, who also longed to see Jesus. However, because Zacchaeus was very short, he climbed a sycamore tree beside the road in order to get a better view. When Jesus arrived, he stopped under the tree and looked up. "Come down, Zacchaeus," he said, "I'd like to stay at your house." People were amazed that Jesus wanted to be with someone like Zacchaeus, and Zacchaeus was overwhelmed by Jesus' love. After supper, he declared that he would give half his possessions to the poor. Jesus replied, "Today salvation has come to this house."

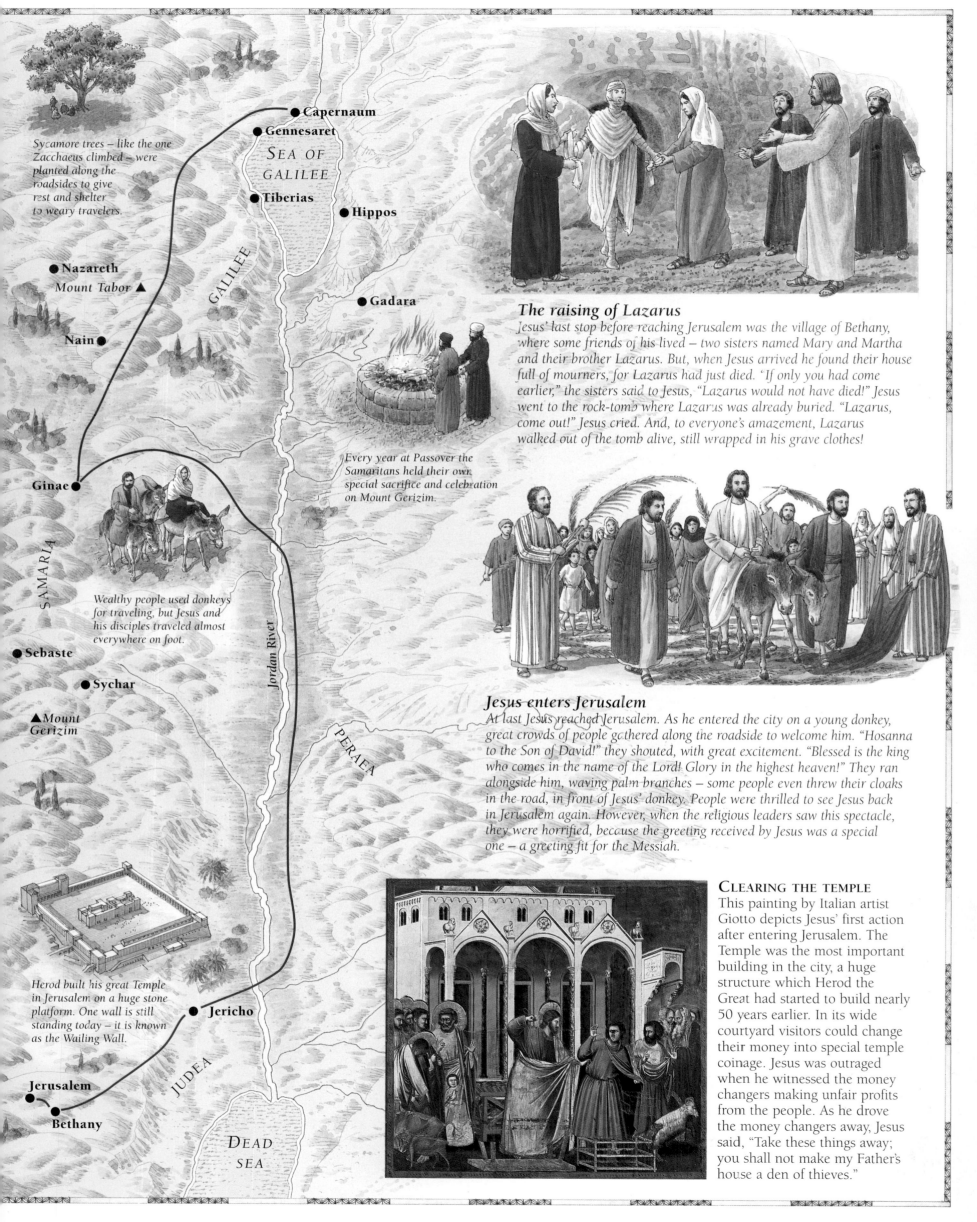

Capernaum
Gennesaret
SEA OF
GALILEE
Tiberias
Hippos

GALILEE

Sycamore trees – like the one Zacchaeus climbed – were planted along the roadsides to give rest and shelter to weary travelers.

Nazareth
Mount Tabor ▲

Nain

Gadara

Every year at Passover the Samaritans held their own special sacrifice and celebration on Mount Gerizim.

SAMARIA

Ginae

Wealthy people used donkeys for traveling, but Jesus and his disciples traveled almost everywhere on foot.

Sebaste

Sychar

▲Mount
Gerizim

Jordan River

PERAEA

Herod built his great Temple in Jerusalem on a huge stone platform. One wall is still standing today – it is known as the Wailing Wall.

Jericho

JUDEA

Jerusalem

Bethany

DEAD
SEA

The raising of Lazarus

Jesus' last stop before reaching Jerusalem was the village of Bethany, where some friends of his lived – two sisters named Mary and Martha and their brother Lazarus. But, when Jesus arrived he found their house full of mourners, for Lazarus had just died. 'If only you had come earlier,' the sisters said to Jesus, 'Lazarus would not have died!' Jesus went to the rock-tomb where Lazarus was already buried. 'Lazarus, come out!' Jesus cried. And, to everyone's amazement, Lazarus walked out of the tomb alive, still wrapped in his grave clothes!

Jesus enters Jerusalem

At last Jesus reached Jerusalem. As he entered the city on a young donkey, great crowds of people gathered along the roadside to welcome him. "Hosanna to the Son of David!" they shouted, with great excitement. "Blessed is the king who comes in the name of the Lord! Glory in the highest heaven!" They ran alongside him, waving palm branches – some people even threw their cloaks in the road, in front of Jesus' donkey. People were thrilled to see Jesus back in Jerusalem again. However, when the religious leaders saw this spectacle, they were horrified, because the greeting received by Jesus was a special one – a greeting fit for the Messiah.

CLEARING THE TEMPLE

This painting by Italian artist Giotto depicts Jesus' first action after entering Jerusalem. The Temple was the most important building in the city, a huge structure which Herod the Great had started to build nearly 50 years earlier. In its wide courtyard visitors could change their money into special temple coinage. Jesus was outraged when he witnessed the money changers making unfair profits from the people. As he drove the money changers away, Jesus said, "Take these things away; you shall not make my Father's house a den of thieves."

41

JESUS' DEATH AND RESURRECTION

AT THE END OF THEIR LONG JOURNEY, Jesus and his disciples stood on the Mount of Olives and looked across the Kidron Valley at Jerusalem. Much of this beautiful city had been rebuilt during the reign of Roman ruler Herod the Great (37–4 BC), and by the time of Jesus' last visit, Jerusalem was one of the greatest cities in Rome's eastern empire. Many new buildings could be found all over the city, including the Antonia Fortress, built on the northwest corner of Temple Mount. On his arrival Jesus was filled with sadness because he knew that as soon as the Passover festival ended, he would be arrested and killed. Jesus had many enemies in Jerusalem because the Jewish leaders there felt threatened by his increasing popularity. Jesus spent Passover in Jerusalem with his 12 disciples. While they were eating their Passover supper, Jesus announced that one of the disciples would betray him. After this last supper, Jesus and the disciples went to the Garden of Gethsemane, situated on the side of the Mount of Olives, in order to pray and rest. While the disciples slept, Jesus was in great agony and prayed for God to give him strength to go through the ordeal he knew he would soon have to face.

SITE OF THE LAST SUPPER
This building stands on the spot where Jesus may have held his last Passover meal. Here, Jesus used the bread and the wine as vivid symbols of his body and his blood and told his disciples to celebrate the meal in his memory.

Damascus Gate

Possible location of Golgotha, where Jesus was crucified.

Jesus' body was laid in a tomb like this, with a large round stone framing the entrance. Two women found this stone rolled aside, and the tomb empty. Jesus had risen from the dead!

The betrayal
Jesus finished praying late in the evening and eventually returned to his friends who were sleeping in the olive groves. Suddenly, he exclaimed, "Look! Here comes my betrayer." Judas, one of Jesus' 12 disciples, appeared, followed by a crowd carrying swords and burning torches. Judas went up to Jesus and said, "Master!" and gave him a kiss on the cheek. This was the signal the crowd had been waiting for, and immediately two men came forward and arrested Jesus. Judas had been paid thirty pieces of silver by the chief priests for betraying Jesus.

Special spices were used to prepare bodies for burial. Ointments were made and then sealed onto the body with bandages.

Herod's Palace

The trial of Jesus
Jesus was taken to a Jewish court and quickly condemned to die for claiming to be the Son of God. Next, he was taken to Pilate, the Roman governor of Judea, because only Romans could command executions. Jesus' enemies stood outside, shouting for his crucifixion. Pilate stood on the balcony of the Antonia Fortress and told the crowd that Jesus was innocent, but they shouted so loudly that Pilate gave in to their demand. He washed his hands in front of the crowds, to show that he wanted no part in Jesus' death.

Area where Jesus' Last Supper is believed to have taken place.

| 0 | 100 | 200 | 300 Meters |
| 0 | 100 | 200 | 300 Yards |

City walls

The crucifixion

Jesus was stripped of his clothing and dressed in a scarlet robe; then the Roman soldiers mocked him. A crown of twisted thorns was cruelly forced upon his head, and after being beaten, Jesus had to carry his cross through the streets of Jerusalem to Golgotha. At 9 o'clock, Jesus was nailed upon the cross, alongside two criminals. As onlookers shouted insults at him, Jesus said, "Father, forgive them, for they do not know what they do." Mary, Jesus' mother, and Mary Magdalene, his friend, were among the people who watched in sorrow as Jesus drew his last breath. At noon, a great darkness fell over the land, and three hours later, Jesus died. His body was wrapped in clean linen and laid in a tomb cut in the rock.

The Passover meal was one of the highlights of the year. Families remembered the night when the Israelites left Egypt for the Promised Land.

Antonia Fortress

Herod's Temple, where religious leaders discussed plans to kill Jesus.

The Mount of Olives, just to the east of Jerusalem, gave a wonderful view of the city to travelers arriving from Jericho.

KIDRON VALLEY

Court of the Gentiles

Pool of Siloam

STREETS OF JERUSALEM

The street map of Jerusalem has not changed much since the time of Jesus, and it is easy to imagine Jesus and his followers walking these streets. The traditional route of Jesus' last steps through the streets of Jerusalem as he carried his cross to Golgotha is known as the Via Dolorosa, or the Way of Sorrows.

The Resurrection

Two days after Jesus' death and burial, two disciples were traveling to Emmaus, a village near Jerusalem. Suddenly a stranger joined them and asked them why they looked so sad. They told him about Jesus and their lost hopes. To their surprise the stranger said, "You are so foolish! Doesn't the Bible teach that the Messiah will rise again?" At the end of their journey, the two disciples realized that the stranger was Jesus and rushed to Jerusalem to tell people that they had seen the Lord.

The ascension

Over a period of six weeks, Jesus appeared to the disciples several times in Jerusalem and Galilee. He told them that they must spread the message of God's kingdom, as he had done. He said that God would give them power to do this, by sending his Holy Spirit to them. Finally, Jesus led the disciples to a mountain in Galilee. "All authority in heaven and on earth has been given to me," he said. "Go and make disciples of all nations, baptizing them. And surely I am with you always." Then he rose out of sight into a cloud above them. As the disciples watched Jesus disappear, two men dressed in white appeared, and told them that Jesus would one day return in the same way.

THE EARLY CHURCH

BEFORE HE ASCENDED TO HEAVEN, Jesus gave his disciples a promise. "When the Holy Spirit has come upon you, you will receive power and will tell people about me everywhere in Jerusalem, throughout Judea, in Samaria, and to the ends of the Earth." Soon after Jesus' ascension, the disciples received the Holy Spirit, on the day of Pentecost. Boldly they began to speak about Jesus all over Jerusalem. Many people were convinced when they heard about Jesus' resurrection. Quickly the message spread and soon there were thousands of Jews who believed that Jesus was the true Messiah. Some Jews, however, were horrified, particularly those who had been Jesus' enemies. They began to arrest Jesus' followers and even killed some of them. One of these opponents was a Pharisee named Saul. He hated Christians, as the followers of Jesus were now called. However, when Jesus appeared to him, Saul became a fearless missionary on his behalf. Based in the church at Antioch in Syria, Saul made several missionary journeys spreading the word of Jesus all around Asia Minor and Greece. Saul became known by his Greek name, Paul, because he was one of the first to bring the Christian message to non-Jewish people.

The whole Roman Empire was crisscrossed by excellent roads, which made traveling much easier for the first Christian missionaries.

PAUL'S JOURNEY TO DAMASCUS
PAUL'S FIRST JOURNEY AD 45
PAUL'S SECOND JOURNEY AD 50
PAUL'S THIRD JOURNEY AD 55
PAUL'S JOURNEY TO ROME AD 60

0   50   100   150   200   250 Kilometers
0   50   100   150 Miles

Paul's shipwreck
On his journeys, Paul had made many enemies who wanted him to be arrested and executed. Eventually, Paul was taken as a prisoner to Rome – to appear before the emperor Nero. The ship's captain decided to risk a dangerous autumn crossing from Crete to Italy. Then disaster struck – a great northeasterly wind blew up, and the ship was driven helplessly for fourteen days until it reached the coast of Malta. God assured Paul that no lives would be lost, and all 276 people on board got safely to shore.

THE PRISON AT PHILIPPI
Philippi is one of the most well-preserved ancient Greek cities. Visitors today can see what may be the remains of the prison where Paul and his friend Silas were held captive on Paul's second journey. Paul's preaching in Philippi had created enemies, which led to his and Silas' arrest. One night, as the two men prayed and sang to God, an earthquake shook the walls, releasing their chains and springing open the prison door.

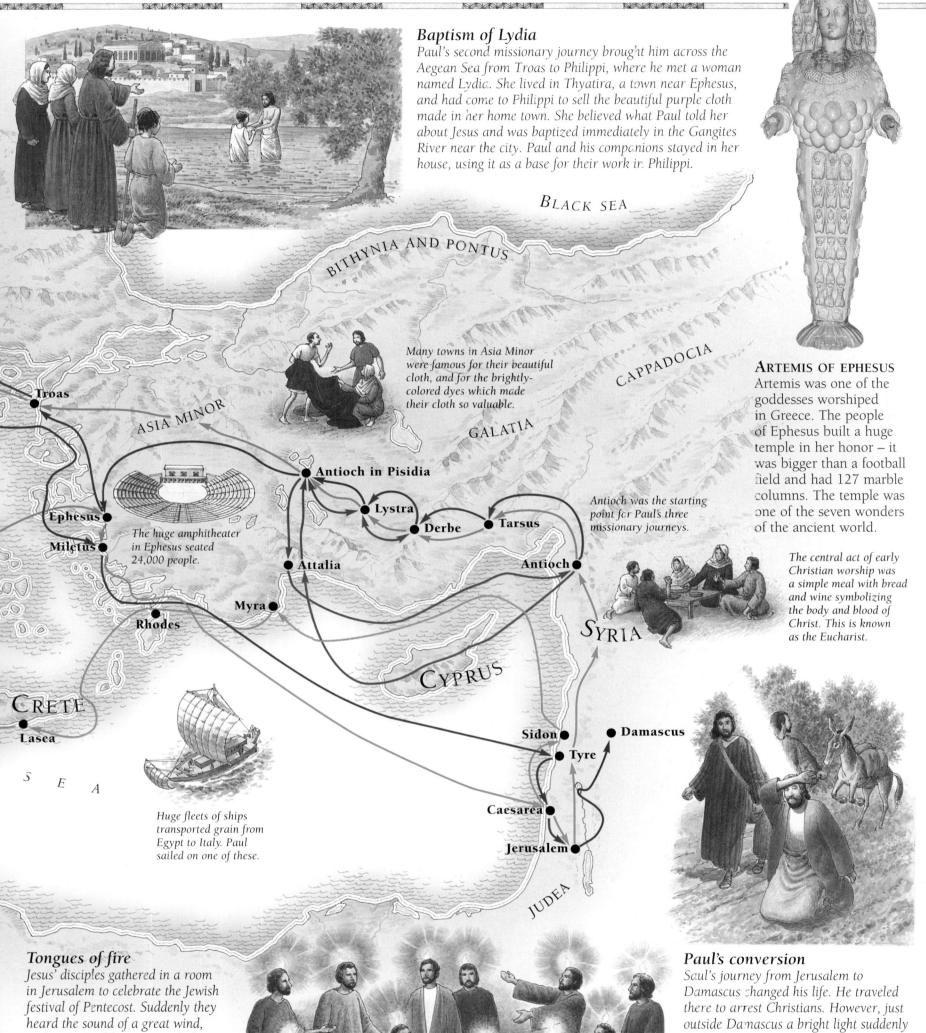

Baptism of Lydia

Paul's second missionary journey brought him across the Aegean Sea from Troas to Philippi, where he met a woman named Lydia. She lived in Thyatira, a town near Ephesus, and had come to Philippi to sell the beautiful purple cloth made in her home town. She believed what Paul told her about Jesus and was baptized immediately in the Gangites River near the city. Paul and his companions stayed in her house, using it as a base for their work in Philippi.

BLACK SEA

BITHYNIA AND PONTUS

Many towns in Asia Minor were famous for their beautiful cloth, and for the brightly-colored dyes which made their cloth so valuable.

CAPPADOCIA

GALATIA

ASIA MINOR

Troas

The huge amphitheater in Ephesus seated 24,000 people.

Ephesus

Miletus

Antioch in Pisidia

Lystra

Derbe

Tarsus

Antioch was the starting point for Paul's three missionary journeys.

Attalia

Antioch

Myra

SYRIA

Rhodes

CYPRUS

ARTEMIS OF EPHESUS

Artemis was one of the goddesses worshiped in Greece. The people of Ephesus built a huge temple in her honor – it was bigger than a football field and had 127 marble columns. The temple was one of the seven wonders of the ancient world.

The central act of early Christian worship was a simple meal with bread and wine symbolizing the body and blood of Christ. This is known as the Eucharist.

CRETE

Lasea

S E A

Huge fleets of ships transported grain from Egypt to Italy. Paul sailed on one of these.

Sidon

Damascus

Tyre

Caesarea

Jerusalem

JUDEA

Tongues of fire

Jesus' disciples gathered in a room in Jerusalem to celebrate the Jewish festival of Pentecost. Suddenly they heard the sound of a great wind, and tongues of fire appeared above their heads. It was the sign that the Holy Spirit was with them. The disciples began to speak in other languages. People had come to Jerusalem from other countries for the festival. They were amazed to hear the apostles talking about God's love in their own language.

Paul's conversion

Saul's journey from Jerusalem to Damascus changed his life. He traveled there to arrest Christians. However, just outside Damascus a bright light suddenly flashed, and Saul heard a voice: "Saul, Saul, why are you persecuting me?" "Who are you, sir?" Saul asked. "I am Jesus, the one you are persecuting!" the voice answered. "Now get up and go into the city. You will be told what you are to do." Saul became a Christian, and one of the greatest missionaries and thinkers of the Christian Church.

A-Z OF BIBLE PLACES

THE EVENTS OF THE BIBLE TAKE place in the Middle East. From Abraham, who was born in Ur, in southern Iraq, to nearly 2,000 years later with apostle Paul, who completed his career in Rome, the capital of the Roman Empire, the Bible is full of exciting stories. There are 2,175 miles (3,500 km) between Ur in the east and Rome in the west. Between them lie Syria, Lebanon, Turkey, Israel, and Greece, with Egypt to the south. This is where much of the Bible takes place, around the land of Israel and the ancient city of Jerusalem. In this A-Z you will find the main places mentioned in the Bible.

AMMON
A country to the east of the Dead Sea. The Israelites passed through Ammon on their way to the Promised Land.

ANTIOCH
This city in Syria was one of the largest cities in the world at the time of Jesus. It was the place where followers of Jesus were first called "Christians."

ASHDOD
One of the five chief cities of the Philistines. Ashdod was the biggest, with its own port nearby and a huge statue of the god Dagon.

ASHKELON
Another Philistine city, on the coast between Jaffa and Gaza. King Herod the Great was born here.

ASSYRIA
An ancient kingdom east of Palestine which became a mighty empire in the 8th and 7th centuries BC. The Assyrian armies captured the northern kingdom of Israel in 721 BC and carried many people into exile from their homes.

ATHENS
The capital and chief city of Greece. Paul preached a famous sermon there.

ATTALIA
The chief port of Pamphylia, on the southern coast of Asia Minor.

BABEL
The name of the earliest city on the site of Babylon. Here people tried to build a massive tower up to heaven.

BABYLON
A city on the Euphrates River, 49 miles (80 km) south of Baghdad. It became very powerful as the center of a huge empire. Babylon was most famous for its hanging gardens, which King Nebuchadnezzar built for his wife, Amytis.

BEERSHEBA
An important town about 46 miles (75 km) south-west of Jerusalem. It existed in the time of Abraham and is often referred to as one of the southernmost towns in Israel.

BETHEL
Bethel is the Hebrew word for "House of God," and the name reminded people that God had appeared to Jacob in a dream he had there. Later, Bethel became a religious center.

BETHLEHEM
Just 5.5 miles (9 km) south of Jerusalem, Bethlehem is also known as the City of David, because King David came from there. It is the birthplace of Jesus.

BETHANY
A village on the other side of the Mount of Olives, 1.8 miles (3 km) from Jerusalem.

BETHSAIDA
A village at the northern end of the Sea of Galilee, which Jesus often visited. Three of his disciples – Peter, Andrew, and Philip – came from here.

CAESAREA PHILIPPI
A town in the far north of Palestine, nestled at the foot of Mount Hermon. Herod's son Philip, who ruled this area, called it Caesarea after Roman emperor Caesar Augustus.

CANA
The village in Galilee where Jesus performed his first miracle – turning the water into wine.

CANAAN
The name of the land of Israel before the Israelite tribes entered it after their long journey from Egypt. This land was promised to the Israelites from God.

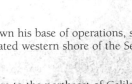

CAPERNAUM
Jesus made this town his base of operations, situated on the densely populated western shore of the Sea of Galilee.

CARMEL
The mountain range to the northeast of Galilee, situated near the Mediterranean coast. Here, Elijah challenged the prophets of Baal.

COLOSSAE
Paul wrote one of his New Testament letters to the church in this little town, which was up the valley of the Lycus River, not far from Ephesus.

CORINTH
One of the chief cities of Greece. Here Paul lived for nearly two years, preaching about Jesus and founding the church. It was a very busy trading city, home to people from all over the Mediterranean.

DAMASCUS
The chief city of Syria in New Testament times and today. It is a very old city, known to Abraham, and it is mentioned throughout the Bible. Paul became a Christian on the road to Damascus, and then had to escape from the city by being lowered from the city wall in a basket.

DEAD SEA
A lake between Israel and Jordan, the surface of which is the lowest place on earth – 1400 ft (427 m) below sea level.

DOTHAN
A town south of Mount Carmel. Here, Joseph's brothers sold him to Ishmaelite traders on their way to Egypt.

EDOM
The country south of the Dead Sea. It belonged to Israel under David and Solomon, but later became independent.

EGYPT
The large country in the northeast corner of Africa. Ninety-six percent of Egypt is desert and nearly all its people live in the four percent of habitable land on either side of the Nile River. The Israelites lived there until the Exodus, under Moses' leadership.

EKRON
One of the five great Philistine cities. It was only 22 miles (35 km) west of Jerusalem, so the Israelites often felt threatened, having enemies living so close to them.

ENGEDI
An important oasis and freshwater spring west of the Dead Sea. David hid there when he was running from Saul.

EPHESUS
One of the biggest cities in the world in the time of Paul, who spent over two years there preaching about Jesus.

EUPHRATES
The longest river in western Asia, sometimes just called "the river" in the Bible. Palestine was part of the Persian province called "Beyond the River" – that is, west of the Euphrates.

GADARA
The place where Jesus healed a demon-possessed man. Unfortunately, we do not know exactly where Gadara was.

GALATIA
The area in southern Asia Minor which Paul and Barnabas visited on their first missionary journey.

GALILEE
A lake and a region in northern Israel. Jesus grew up here and spent much of his ministry in the many towns and cities of this region. The Sea of Galilee (actually a lake) is mentioned in many of the Gospel stories in the Bible.

GATH
One of the five Philistine cities. The giant Goliath, whom David killed with a stone, came from Gath.

GETHSEMANE
The garden on the side of the Mount of Olives where Jesus prayed on the night he was betrayed and arrested.

GILBOA
The mountain in the territory of Issachar, in north Palestine, where King Saul and his sons were killed by the Philistines.

GILEAD
A large area east of the Jordan valley, extending north of the Dead Sea where the tribes of Reuben, Gad, and Manasseh settled.

GOSHEN
The fertile area in the Nile Delta where the Israelites lived during their time in Egypt. Goshen was saved from the plagues suffered by the rest of Egypt just before the Exodus.

GREECE
Following the victories of the Greek king Alexander the Great, Greece supplied a common language and culture to the whole of the eastern Mediterranean, including Israel.

HARAN
A town in present-day southeast Turkey. Abraham lived in Haran, before moving south into Canaan.

HAZOR
This city in northern Palestine was the largest Canaanite city when Joshua and the Israelites conquered the land. Hazor was destroyed by the Assyrians in the 8th century BC.

HEBRON

The highest town in Palestine, Hebron was just 19 miles (30 km) from Jerusalem. Here, Abraham, Isaac, and Jacob were buried, and King David began his reign here – it was his capital before he captured Jerusalem.

HERMON

This great mountain north of Galilee, rising to 9,232 ft (2814 m), separates Israel from Syria. Jesus' Transfiguration may have taken place here.

ISRAEL

The country and the nation at the heart of the Bible. Sometimes this name is used for the whole people, sometimes just for the ten-tribe northern kingdom.

JERICHO

A town west of the Jordan River, Jericho was the first great walled city of Canaan, conquered by Joshua and the Israelites. It is one of the oldest cities in the world.

JERUSALEM

The capital of Israel since about 1000 BC, when King David settled there and united the nation. Since that time, Jerusalem became the "holy city" for the Jews, and later for the Christians and the Muslims. The name means "city of peace," but it has often been surrounded by war.

JORDAN RIVER

The Jordan rises in the north on Mount Hermon, fed by the snow there, and flows down the Jordan Valley to the Dead Sea.

JUDEA

This was the Greek and Roman name for Palestine. In the time of Paul the Roman province of Judea included Judah and Jerusalem in the south, Samaria, and Galilee. The "Wilderness of Judea" mentioned in reference to John the Baptist is the desert west of the Dead Sea.

LACHISH

A large Canaanite town, 30 miles (48 km) southwest of Jerusalem, taken over by the Israelites. It was turned into a fort, but later captured by the Assyrians.

LYSTRA

A remote city in the Roman province of Galatia (near Konya in Turkey). Paul and Barnabas visited this town on their first missionary journey. Here, Paul healed a crippled man, but was stoned and nearly killed. Some of the people of Lystra became Christians and Paul returned to visit.

MACEDONIA

The kingdom in northern Greece from which King Alexander the Great came. Paul dreamed about a man asking him to come to Macedonia and help them. Paul made the visit on his second missionary journey.

MASADA

The fortress near the Dead Sea where the Jews held out against the Roman army in AD 73.

MEGGIDO

A large ancient city near Mount Carmel. The Canaanite king of Meggido was defeated by Joshua when the Israelites conquered Canaan. Later, King Josiah died there, fighting the Egyptians. During his reign, Solomon chose it as one of his fortified towns.

MESOPOTAMIA

This Greek name means "between the rivers." It describes the ancient area between the Tigris and Euphrates Rivers, which contained some of the world's oldest cities, including Babylon, Nineveh, and Ur, Abraham's birthplace.

MIDIAN

The Midianites were nomadic people who lived south of Palestine, way down in the Sinai Peninsula. They were famous for the camels they bred. Moses' wife, Zipporah, was a Midianite.

MOAB

Moab was the country situated on a high plateau of land east of the Dead Sea. The Moabites were often enemies of Israel, but the book of Ruth tells the story of how a Moabite girl came to live in Bethlehem.

NAIN

The village in Galilee where Jesus stopped a funeral procession and brought a young man back to life.

NAZARETH

The town in Galilee where Jesus grew up and worked with his father, Joseph, as a carpenter.

NILE RIVER

The Nile River flows from Lake Victoria, in Tanzania, 3,480 miles (5,600 km) north of the Mediterranean. It gives life to Egypt, supplying water to grow crops in the desert. Its water turned to blood in one of the ten plagues that took place before the Exodus.

NIMRUD

Nimrud is the modern name of the ancient city of Calah, or Kalhu. one of the chief cities of the Assyrian Empire. It lay beside the Tigris River, just south of Nineveh.

NINEVEH

The capital of Assyria, and of the Assyrian Empire, built beside the Tigris River in northern Iraq. Nineveh ... powerful city, but fell to the Babylonians in 612 BC, ... edicted by the prophet Zephaniah. The site of the ... goes back to about 4500 BC.

ERSIA

Cyrus king of Persia, conquered the Babylonians in 540 ..., and the Persian Empire then grew until it covered most of the known world. The empire was divided into 127 provinces, and great roads were built to hold the empire together. It was King Cyrus who allowed exiled Jews to return to their homelands.

PHILIPPI

A large town, and also a Roman colony, on the coast of Macedonia, where many retired Roman soldiers lived. Paul visited Philippi as part of his mission.

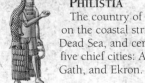

PHILISTIA

The country of the Philistines. It was on the coastal strip west of Judah and the Dead Sea, and centered on the Philistines' five chief cities: Ashkelon, Gaza, Ashdod, Gath, and Ekron.

QUMRAN

An area near the Dead Sea, famous for the discovery of the Dead Sea scrolls found there. These scrolls were part of the library of a Jewish monastic community.

RED SEA

The arm of the sea that separates Egypt and northeast Africa from Arabia. In the Bible it is sometimes called the "Reed Sea."

ROME

The capital of the Roman Empire in Italy. Roman armies first invaded Palestine in 63 BC, and from then onward the country was ruled by Rome – either directly, by governors like Pilate, or indirectly, through the Herods. Jews generally hated Roman rule.

SAMARIA

Capital of the Northern Kingdom of Israel, built by King Omri to rival Jerusalem. His son King Ahab continued the building. Samaria fell to the Assyrians in c. 722 BC and it was later rebuilt by King Herod, who renamed it Sebaste.

SHEBA

Now called Yemen, in southwest Arabia. In the 10th century BC the Queen of Sheba visited King Solomon to test his wisdom.

SHECHEM

An ancient town in central Palestine, about 31 miles (50 km) north of Jerusalem. Abraham stayed in Shechem, Joshua gathered all the tribes of Israel here, and later, the northern tribes rejected King Rehoboam here.

SIDON

Originally founded by the Phoenicians to provide a harbor on the north Palestine coast (today it is in Lebanon). It is mentioned throughout the Bible – Jezebel was the daughter of the king of Sidon and in the New Testament Jesus visited Sidon and the neighboring city of Tyre.

SINAI

The mountain in Arabia where God gave the Law to Moses. Unfortunately. we do not know for sure which mountain this was. It is also the name of a peninsula and a desert.

SUSA

One of the great cities of the Persian Empire. Darius I built a lavish palace here, the remains of which can still be seen today.

TARSUS

The city near the coast of Cicilia (southern Turkey) where Paul was born. He called it "no ordinary city."

THESSALONICA

The chief city of Macedonia (northern Greece). Here, Paul preached on his second missionary journey, and wrote two of his New Testament letters to the church.

TIBERIAS

Herod Antipas built Tiberias, on the western shore of the Sea of Galilee, to be his capital. He named it after the Roman emperor Tiberias.

TYRE

Large port 25 miles (40 km) south of Sidon. King Hiram of Tyre supplied many of the materials for Solomon's Temple in Jerusalem. In New Testament times, Jesus visited and preached in Tyre.

UR

This city in ancient Mesopotamia or Chaldea (now southern Iraq) is famous for its ziggurat (a rectangular temple tower). Birthplace of Abraham.

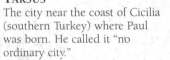

INDEX

Biblical references are added in italics so that you can read more about your favorite stories and places in the Bible.

Acknowledgments

Dorling Kindersley would like to thank the following:
Peter Radcliffe, Julia Harris, and Vicky Wharton for design assistance; Martin Redfern, and Scarlett O'Hara for editorial assistance; Amanda Russell, Mollie Gillard, Sally Hamilton, and Rachel Hilford for additional picture research; Simon Mumford for map consultancy; and Chris Bernstein for the index. Many thanks also to Rupert Chapman and Felicity Cobbing at the Palestine Exploration Fund.

Picture Credits
Abbreviations key: r=right, l=left, t=top, c=center, b=below

AKG London: Erich Lessing 24tr, 33bc. 30tr. **Ancient Art & Architecture Collection:** 8–9tc. **A.S.A.P. Ltd:** 36tr; Eyal Bartov 4–5; Lev Borodulin 18tc, Douglas Guthrie 24cl; Garo Nalbandian 9cr, 35tl,41tr. **Bridgeman Art Library, London/New York:** *Tower of Babel*, 1563 (oil on panel) (for details see 93768-69) by Pieter the Elder Brueghel (c. 1515–69), Kunsthistorisches Museum, Vienna, Austria 33cr, *Christ Calling His Disciples*, 1839 (oil on canvas) by Adam Brenner (1800–91) New Walk Museum, Leicester City Museum, UK 39.

British Museum, London: 5br, 8cl, 8bl, 9bc, 9bc, 9br. 14tl, 14br, 16bl, 20ca, 32tc, 35cr. **British Library:** 22br; **Corbis:** 8cb; Dave Bartruff; 16cr. **Sonia Halliday Photographs:** 19tl, 42tr, 43ca, 44bc, 45tr; T C Rising 31tr. **Robert Harding Picture Library:** 6bc; E. Simanor 7bl. **Zev Radovan, Jerusalem:** 6br, 14bl, 17br, 21tl, 22tr, 26cla, 39tr. **Scala Group S.p.A.:** 41bc. **Topham Picturepoint:** 23cr, 27cra. **Art Directors & TRIP:** R. Cracknell 6cl, 17cra. I. Genut 12-13; M. Jelliffe 16tr; J. Stanley 36–37. **Palestine Exploration Fund:** 9tr, reproduced by kind permission of the Palestine Exploration Fund.